Building a Better World in Your Backyard

After you've read the book,
write your name here and pass it on:

_____

_____

_____

_____

_____

_____

_____

_____

_____

_____

Other works by Paul Wheaton:

World Domination Gardening (3-DVD set)[1]

Building a Cob Style Rocket Mass Heater (DVD)[2]

Better Wood Heat: DIY Rocket Mass Heaters (8-DVD set)[3]

Permaculture Playing Cards[4]

Permaculture Design Course (100-hour recording)[5]

Appropriate Technology Course (77-hour recording)[5]

Rocket Ovens: More Than a Wood-Fired Pizza Oven (DVD)[6]

Homesteading and Permaculture Podcasts (over 400)[7]

permies.com

richsoil.com

youtube.com/paulwheaton

1 permies.com/t/52912
2 permies.com/t/60211
3 permies.com/t/63837
4 permies.com/t/57503
5 permies.com/t/65386
6 permies.com/t/90191
7 permies.com/f/88

Building a Better World in Your Backyard

Instead of Being Angry at Bad Guys

Paul Wheaton & Shawn Klassen-Koop

The information in this book is condensed from a larger body of work. As a result, this book conveys ideas, but is not a complete "how to" guide and should not be taken as such. For full details on how to follow through with these ideas, please do your own research. For anything you choose to do as a result of reading this book, the complete list of things that anybody involved in creating this book is obligated to do is:

possibly point and laugh

First edition, 2019. Printed in the USA.

Cover design, illustrations, and formatting by Tracy Wandling

For errata, suggestions for a second edition, reviews, and comments: permies.com/bwb

buildingabetterworldbook.com   permies.com   richsoil.com

Publisher's Cataloging-in-Publication Data

Names: Wheaton, Paul, author. | Klassen-Koop, Shawn, author.
Title: Building a better world in your backyard , instead of being angry at bad guys / Paul Wheaton ; Shawn Klassen-Koop.
Description: Includes bibliographical references. | Winkler, Manitoba: Shawn Klassen-Koop, 2019.
Identifiers: ISBN 9781999171407 (pbk.) | 9781999171421 (PDF ebook) | 9781-999171438 (EPUB) | 9781999171445 (MOBI) | 9781999171414 (audiobook)
Subjects: LCSH Sustainable living. | Climate change mitigation. | Human ecology. | Self-reliant living. | Urban homesteading. | Permaculture. | Sustainable agriculture. | Home economics. | Conservation of natural resources. | Environmentalism. | Environmental protection – Citizen participation. | BISAC HOUSE & HOME / Sustainable Living | REFERENCE / Personal & Practical Guides
Classification: LCC TD171.7 .W43 2019 | DDC 363.7 – dc23

to Lawton Emerson McDaniel

for caring for a broken boy

~ Paul

to Andrea

without whose support this book would not exist

~ Shawn

"Without deviation from the norm,
progress is not possible."
~ Frank Zappa

Table of Contents

Part 0: Introduction   1
Chapter 1: A Different Approach to Solving World Problems   2

Part 1: The Problems   5
Chapter 2: Environmentalist vs "Environmentalist"   6
    The Wheaton Eco-Poser Test   6
Chapter 3: The Wicked Lies About Light Bulbs   8
    Free Light Bulbs! Love and Kisses from China!   9
    Legally Pump Stimulants into Your Employees All Day with Blue Light!   9
    The Cartel That Rigged the Light Bulb Game   10
    It Says "Eco" on the Label – They Forgot to Mention "Carcinogenic"   11
    Big Energy Savings! (Except in Cold Climates)   12
    The Ultimate Example of Greenwashing   13
Chapter 4: Carbon Footprint   14
Chapter 5: Petroleum Footprint   17
Chapter 6: Toxic Footprint   20

Part 2: General Strategies   23
Chapter 7: The Wheaton Eco Scale   24
Chapter 8: Moving Way Beyond Recycling   27
    Attack of the Pizza Box   27
    Recycling 2.0, 3.0, 4.0, and 5.0   28
Chapter 9: Vote with Your Wallet   30
Chapter 10: Radically Deviant Financial Strategies   32
    The Story of Gert: A Millionaire Life Without a Million Dollars   32
    Owning a Home Without Grovelling to a Bank   34
    Early Retirement Extreme   35
    Give a Gift to Your Future Self with Passive Income Streams   35
    The BEER Plan   37
    A Clever Recipe for More Luxuriant Living at Half the Cost   37
    A Few Experiments Being Conducted on Human Beings   38
Chapter 11: Organic vs Local   39
Chapter 12: Vegan vs Omnivore vs Junk Food   41
    VORP – Expanding Our Vocabulary to Value Garden Food over Diet Cola   42
    When a Vegan Diet Has a Lower Carbon Footprint. And When It Doesn't.   44
    GAT: Government-Mandated Acceptable Levels of Toxicity   45

Part 3: Within the Walls of Your Home   47
Chapter 13: REALLY Reducing Home Energy Usage   48
    63% of Home Energy Use in a Cold Climate Is Heat   49
        How I Cut 87% off My Electric Heat Bill and Stayed Toasty Warm   49
        The New Wood Heat: Smokeless and One Tenth the Wood   51
    19% of Home Energy Use is Hot Water   54
        Boom Squish   54
        Making Your Hot Water Tank More Efficient   54

Saving Hot Water Without Suffering Another Cold Shower   55

5% of Home Energy Use is Lighting   56

3% of Home Energy Use is Laundry   56

The Little Things   58

The Physical Energy Footprint per Adult   58

Chapter 14: More People Living Under One Roof Without Stabbing Each Other   60

"Obey or Else"   61

The Knives are in the Kitchen   61

Dirty Cup CSI   62

Chapter 15: Toxic Gick vs 20 Years of Your Life   64

A Better Cleaning Strategy Than Replacing Dirt with Poison   64

Cast Iron Can Be Nonstick; Teflon Is Always Poison   65

Going Pooless   66

Bug Killer You Can Eat!   67

Part 4: More Than Half of Each Footprint Can Be Resolved in a Backyard   69

Chapter 16: The Huge Link Between Food and Global Footprints (Vegans Too!)   70

Chapter 17: Double the Food with One Tenth of the Effort   72

Transplanting? That's Unnecessary Work!   73

Prepping the Soil to Not Need Prepping   74

Planting Once and Harvesting for Years   75

Mulching 2.0: Being Naked Is No Longer Required!   75

3D Gardening – Big Berms Bring Big Benefits   77

How Trees Nurture Gardens, Cool Your Home, Heat Your Home, and Save the World   78

Replacing Fertilizer with Polyculture   79

Monocrops Need Pest Control; Nature Doesn't   80

Let's Do the Math   81

Chapter 18: The Dark Side of Native Plant Enthusiasm   83

Native to When?   83

Past Invasives Are Now "Native." When Will Current Invasives Become "Native"?   84

The Shifting Definitions of "Noxious Weeds"   84

Lipstick on a Pig: Native Plant Organizations and Herbicide Companies   85

Myth: Native Plants Will Perform Better in Your Area   85

Native-Plant Enthusiasts Eat Only Native Crops, Right?   85

One Person Managing 20,000 Acres vs One Person Managing 10 Acres   86

The Pow Wow Grounds in Elmo, Montana   86

Chapter 19: 20 Things to Do with the Twigs That Fall in Your Yard   87

Chapter 20: Not Composting   90

Chapter 21: Better Than Solar Panels: A Solar Food Dehydrator   92

My Quick Tips for Making a "Down Draft" Solar Food Dehydrator   92

A Natural Recipe for Solar Dehydrator "Black"   93

A Few Things You Can Do with a Solar Dehydrator   93

Chapter 22: Breaking the Toxic Water Cycle with Greywater Recycling   94

A Quickie Greywater System   95

Building a Simple Greywater System   96

Cold Climate Greywater Systems   96

Becoming a Certified Environmentalist   97

Chapter 23: Harvesting Electricity in Your Backyard   98

Chapter 24: The Conventional Lawn vs a Mowable Meadow 101
    Battle for the Sun Deathmatch! Rig the Game for Grass! 101
    Tough Training Leads to Strong Grasses with Deep, Resilient Roots! 103
    Deep, Rich, Magnificent Soil vs Thin, Pathetic Dirt 104
    Free Fertilizers Stomp the Poopies out of the Commercial Offerings 104
    Long-Term Soil vs Short-Term Fertilizer 105
    Bringing in the REAL Professionals (Hint: They Don't Wear Clothes) 105

Part 5: Counter the Footprint of 20 People on a Homestead 107
Chapter 25: How Vegans Benefit from Caring for Cattle, Chickens, Hogs, Etc. 108
    Contemplations in Pampering an Animal 109
    How to Get Five Times More Garden Growth by Gardening with Animals 110
    Building Your Soul with a Plethora of Life Instead of Zappity Zap Zap 111
    If It Smells Bad, You're Doing It Wrong: Never Mucking out a Shelter Again 112
    The Very Best Predator Control Is Not a Fence 112
Chapter 26: Replacing Petroleum with People 114
Chapter 27: Wrestling with Poop Beasts and Peeing in the Garden 117
    Creating a Magnificent Jungle with Your Urine 117
    An Exploration of Pooping Contraptions 118
        Making Poop Jerky and Saving It for Later 120
        Feeding Poop Beasts, Killing Them, and Building Stuff out of Their Bones 121
Chapter 28: The Solutions to Colony Collapse Disorder Are Embarrassingly Simple 123
Chapter 29: Destroy Your Orchard to Make a Food Forest 127
Chapter 30: A Building Design That Solves Almost Everything 130
    Setting Our Design Criteria Extremely High 131
        We Can Do Better Than Straw Bale Designs 131
        We Can Do Better Than Cob Designs 131
        The Dirty Secret of "Sustainable" Building 132
        The Joy and Heartbreak of Earthships 132
        Prevent Wildfires by Building a Home 133
    From Junk to Genius with One Simple Design Change 133
    A Freaky-Cheap Home That Doesn't Look Freaky-Cheap 136
    Using the Heat from Summer to Heat Your Home During the Winter 138
    The Strict Definition of "Wofati" 139
    A Modification for a Year-Round Freezer 139
Chapter 31: Natural Swimming Pools 141
    Keeping the Water Clean 141
    Avoiding the Ice Bath 143
    How Do I Build One? Gimmie! Gimmie Now! 144

Part 6: Conclusion 147
Chapter 32: Hey! You Know What Would be Cool? 148

Appendices 151
Appendix A: World Domination 152
Appendix B: Tabular Summary of Solutions 153
Acknowledgments 157
About the Authors 165

Part 0
Introduction

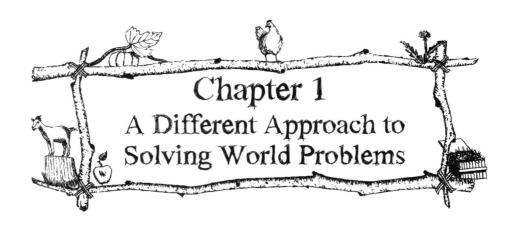

Chapter 1
A Different Approach to Solving World Problems

"It was the best of times, it was the worst of times, it was the age of wisdom, it was the age of foolishness, it was the epoch of belief, it was the epoch of incredulity, it was the season of Light, it was the season of Darkness, it was the spring of hope, it was the winter of despair…"

- Charles Dickens, *A Tale of Two Cities*, 1859

It is the best of times. We have the internet, cars, jets, space travel, movies, electricity, and comforts for the masses far beyond the imagination of Dickens.

It is the worst of times. Political debate continues on whether the human species will survive climate change. Mercury in the atmosphere has made all fish toxic – even fish found in the most remote wilderness. The palette for toxins has changed – it is more subtle but far more dangerous and varied. We now have massive patches of garbage in our oceans, and we continue to route sewage laden with toxic waste into many of our waterways. Cancer now kills 100 times more people, per capita, than during the smoky days of Dickens.[1] War, starvation, and poverty have yet to be rooted out. We now have a collection of new illnesses we are struggling to understand. Most of our electronics have the shame of modern slavery woven into them, and our addiction to these toys forfeits our privacy to a variety of nefarious entities. Not to mention we…

Sorry about that. I have now smacked the "pause" button on the dark stuff. The list still runs on for a few hours, but it was twisting my innards and I think you get the general vibe: the list of global problems is massive and overwhelming.

When confronted with such significant problems, our first instinct is to tell the bad guys to stop being bad. Of course, we'd be doing so on a rigged playing field. And for each person who actually does write a letter or confront the bad guys, there might be a hundred people who simply develop an ulcer.

1 permies.com/t/108161 (cancer stats)

About seven years ago, a friend contacted me to tell me he had become obsessed with fracking. He was actively protesting two or three times a week. He lived in Colorado, so I asked him how he heats his home. He responded, "with natural gas." After all of his protesting, it never occurred to him that he was feeding the monster. When I pointed this out to him, his first response was to switch to electric heat. I then pointed out the environmental problems with electric heat, including how natural gas is now being used to generate electricity in his area. So he then contemplated going without any heat at all. Yikes!

For nearly every global problem, there are solutions we can implement in our backyard that save us money and help us live more luxuriant lives. If a few of us do these things and bask in the glow of the opulence and extra cash, others will observe and think "I want extra luxury and money too! Not fair!" So they emulate, and on and on it goes. Then the global problems sort of just dry up and blow away. That's what this book is about.

I think the reason we see so many people angry is that they genuinely care. But they seem to get stuck at being angry. Some people spend a hundred hours a week for twenty years being angry and not much changes. But I think that if you spend a tiny fraction of that time doing the things mentioned in this book, your global positive impact will be a thousand times greater.

This book is one massive, steaming pile of my opinion. Well, our opinion. About 70% of the book is made from articles, podcasts, videos, presentations, and interviews I (Paul) have shared publicly. And then Shawn and I spent the better part of a year polishing it and augmenting it to make it a single, cohesive piece in order to express a collective position. Because these thoughts and experiences were Paul's before Shawn came along, we agreed to maintain the first person presentation. So when you read this book in your head, you can read it in Paul's voice or, at least, what you imagine it sounding like. At the same time, we agreed that there would be no word in this book that Shawn disagreed with unless there was some sort of accompanying note showing his dissent. It turned out there was no need for such a note.

I live in Montana. Shawn lives in Canada. And so a lot of this book is focused on solutions for people living in a cold climate. But, for those who live in warmer climates, I think that there are still some excellent ideas worth contemplating.

The points made in these chapters have been run by thousands of people to be further polished, tested, and contested. We have attempted to go through every sentence of this book many times to make sure that we have properly qualified each statement. That said, it is still possible that there is a stumble or two in these pages.

Making a comprehensive list of the known global problems would fill several books. My thoughts on solving these issues could fill a few hundred books. Shawn and I have agreed to limit our focus to a few global problems, skip past a lot of the explanations, and then hit just the most important points for each solution. About

"Living in the subtropics, I've noticed that almost everything in this book still applies. Even rocket mass heaters can be useful! If you want to make an impact, I recommend this book for any climate."

- Katie Young

a hundred times throughout this book, we wrote "There are about twenty more pages to write here, but we had to cut that out" – and then we cut those words out too. If you want more information on a particular topic or if you want to discuss these topics with thousands of others who are bonkers about this stuff, feel free to check out the links in the footnotes. That said, we believe that if we solve the issues presented in this book, the rest of the world's issues will be well on their way to being solved too.

For me, nearly all of our problems are solved with a recipe composed mostly of homesteading and permaculture. For those new to the term, permaculture is a regenerative design science. Some people have taken this term in directions that I am not comfortable with, but I have chosen to embrace the word anyway because I appreciate its original intentions and how nearly everything I advocate can conveniently fit into one simple, delicious word. I like to think that permaculture provides a more symbiotic relationship with nature so I can be even lazier.

For each global issue, a lot of hype is put into solutions that have far too little impact on the actual problem. In this book, we will provide a metric for each problem so we can chip away at our own personal impact on the globe and, maybe, eventually, even cover the footprint of twenty others.

Let's get to work.

Part 1
The Problems

Chapter 2
Environmentalist vs "Environmentalist"

I once saw a documentary where a wind farm was forbidden by the government because of the local outcry. The woman who led the resistance said "We must all do our part for the environment!" The people who wanted the wind farm said pretty much the same thing. Leaving the real argument aside, I was very interested in a few clues that were given up about this woman's personal life. My impression, based on very limited data, was that she probably considered herself to be an environmentalist. And yet, if there were some sort of super-accurate machine that could measure her eco level based on her actions over the last year, I think she would score poorly. Very poorly.

I suspect that most people who would call themselves an environmentalist would score poorly. The problem isn't that they are nefarious. Or stupid. It's just that the eco information that they have been exposed to is probably some form of greenwashing misinformation – and plenty of it. So, how do you, dear reader, find out if you really are an eco warrior or an unwitting eco poser? Well, I've come up with a quick and simple test.

The complexity of a truly accurate test could fill a library and would change daily as new information and new problems are discovered. The discussion and debate over the quality and validity of the test could fill a hundred more libraries. But since I am seeking something very simple, I came up with a test that is massively permissive. It allows half of the current population of the United States to proudly sport the label "eco" or "environmentalist."

But the gut-wrenching part is that most of the people (yes, more than half) who read this book and are utterly certain that they are "eco" are about to learn that they are, actually, posers. I won't tell. I promise! Don't kill me!

The Wheaton Eco-Poser Test

I am calling this "The Wheaton Eco-Poser Test"[1] instead of "The Eco-Poser Test" so that everybody who fails this test can make their own test, because, obviously, for them, this test was defective. For example, maybe "The Poppins Eco-Poser Test" would heavily favor umbrella-based transportation schemes.

The average American adult spends about $1000 on heat and electricity per year (an average of $83 per month). The test is to spend less than the average. With one

1 permies.com/t/environmentalists

whammy: kids don't count. So, a household with two adults and four kids needs to spend as little as a household with just two adults.

There you go. That's the whole test. If you spend less than that, congratulations! You made it to eco level 1![2] We have sooooo much cool stuff to talk about – like eco levels 2 and 3 and the rest. But, for now, I need to talk to the angry people coming at me with torches, pitchforks, and other sharp things to teach me about peace and love through the art of stabbing.

This simple little test emerged after years and years of struggling to talk to thousands of people about different trains of thought in what it means to be eco. Or to be an environmentalist. I soon learned that some people were adamant that they were eco, and they could prove it to be true by saying it very loudly. Usually, their justification was rooted in now living a life that was 5% more efficient than at some point in their more wasteful past. And they had no idea just how wasteful their lives were. Or still are.

I guess when it comes to energy, it sort of seems "free" until the energy bills come. And there is very little reliable information on what really works and what is just somebody trying to sell you their stuff. So do you spend five times more than your neighbor? Five times less? I think most people would be shocked to learn how much their bathing and laundry habits really cost. And how some very simple changes can save hundreds, or even thousands, of dollars without sacrificing any comfort.[3]

So, let's get a grip on this. Energy use is a great eco metric. Most of our environmental and political problems are rooted in the source of our energy use. So I think people who really care about humanity and the Earth will use less than average. And since we have all of the statistics on average power consumption, a touch of math is all it takes.

2 permies.com/t/scale
3 permies.com/t/conservation

Chapter 3
The Wicked Lies
About Light Bulbs

Light bulb stuff is pretty trivial. But far too many people are utterly certain that decisions about light bulbs are so globally important that they won't consider other solutions. We have to crush this barrier so we can talk about the really substantial stuff.

Many years ago, an interviewer asked me what one thought I would, if I could, put into the heads of all the people in the world. I started thinking about rocket mass heaters, wofati designs, polyculture, removing toxicity, and reducing disease. While these would all have a profound impact on the world, a nauseous feeling set in as I realized my best answer was: "What people have been told about the relationship between light bulbs and the environment is all twisted for the sake of large companies and their profits."

I never wanted to be "the light bulb guy."[1] Really, I didn't. I'd rather be known for much cooler things. At the same time, when I try to talk about all these cooler things, people say "I don't want to hear about that because I already bought the light bulbs." We have seriously got to get past the light bulb thing in order to really start solving the world's problems.

If we are exploring saving energy used for lighting, I think the first step is to explore your lighting habits rather than buying new bulbs. Years ago, when I made my videos about the problems with Compact Fluorescent Light (CFL) bulbs, I was living by myself. I calculated that I spent $8 per year on electricity for lighting. Yes, that is dollars per year and not dollars per month. And all of my light was incandescent.

For many years, the light bulb that would "save the world" was the CFL bulb. I think I have proven that they are awful in a long list of ways. I'll skip past that disaster in this book. If you're still on the CFL train then go read the stuff I wrote at richsoil.com.[2]

It seems like these days people have moved on to LED lighting as the light bulb that will solve all our problems. In this chapter, I will spell out in excruciating detail why I think that in 2019 the most environmentally friendly light bulb remains, in most cases, despite all modern innovation, the incandescent light bulb.[3] Once we've got that covered we can move on to solving the rest of the world's problems.

1 permies.com/t/16335 (light bulb guy)
2 richsoil.com/cfl
3 permies.com/t/led

Free Light Bulbs! Love and Kisses from China!

Right now, nearly every power company in the United States is happy to provide a "free" energy audit. They will typically come to your home, do a five-minute analysis on weather stripping, and then load you up with "free" light bulbs. And if you don't want the "audit" they will gladly just ship you the light bulbs.

Of course, these bulbs are not really free. It's not like the people in China love us so much that they make them and carry them to our houses, complete with a gift note saying "You are so awesome, we wish to illuminate you! xoxo!" The reality is that you are paying for them a different way – either through taxes or the electric bill.

If the goal is to save energy, the power company would save a lot more energy providing you with a clothes line.[4] So why don't they do that? The answer is what you would expect: profit. The light bulb companies have so many different subsidy programs coming from so many different places that they are making serious bank per bulb. The trick is to move the bulbs. And this is the reason the light bulb companies lobbied to ban incandescent light bulbs – their own product.

I feel like this is a lot of wickedness, and I don't want to support this wickedness. And the LED is being set up to be the new CFL. So I have a bit of anti-LED bias right out of the gate.

Legally Pump Stimulants into Your Employees All Day with Blue Light!

Incandescent light has a long, rich history of providing high-quality light.

LED light has a long, rich history of saying "LED light quality is better" and it turns out the comparison was to LED light from a couple years before – which was awful. So, "better" meant "worse than incandescent, but better than earlier attempts at LED."

LED lights have come a long way on this path. There have been some folks who have done spectral analysis on a variety of LED bulbs and have found some that do a very good job of emulating natural daylight. One person doing the analysis claimed that this was the ultimate test – that this is complete proof that a good LED light provides light as good as, or better than, incandescent. After all, natural daylight is helpful in elevating mood, increasing attention span, and improving one's reaction time.

Natural daylight has a lot of high-energy blue light in it. "Cool white" LEDs also produce a lot of blue light. It is this blue light that gives such beneficial effects during the day. That said, we have evolved for many thousands of years without electric lighting. Our bodies are used to following the natural cycles of sunrise and sunset, and the spectral analysis of natural sunset light differs greatly from that of natural daylight.

Natural sunset light has very little blue in it and a lot more orange and red. An overwhelming amount of research has shown that blue light in the evening suppresses the secretion of melatonin, wrecking natural sleep cycles.[5] This is the same reason we're not supposed to look at screens right before bed. Not only does blue light affect sleep, it also affects emotional behaviors and hormone production, and these three things fuel a long list of ailments. Our bodies are being told by the light that it's still daytime!

4 permies.com/t/dryer
5 permies.com/t/82607 (LED quality)

Therefore, while those cool white LEDs might be alright for light quality during the day, their quality in the evenings is greatly diminished. And it's generally during the evenings that we use lights the most.

Note that warm white LEDs have much less blue in them than cool white LEDs. Warm white LEDs use a yellow phosphor coating on the inside of the bulb to shift the blue light closer to the yellow and green parts of the spectrum. This reduces the concerns of the effects of sleep-cycle disruption by evening lighting. That said, the phosphor coating sometimes degrades and starts to allow more blue light out again.

I think that while the research on warm white LEDs promises much better quality than cool white LED light, there may still be some things about light quality that we don't fully understand. I think that besides sitting in the dark after sunset, the next best thing we can do for our bodies is to "extend the sunset." Oddly enough, it turns out that the spectral analysis of natural sunset just so happens to be nearly identical to that of an incandescent light bulb.

Some will naturally wonder why they don't just make LEDs that mimic the incandescent spectrum instead. After all, there are LEDs in all sorts of colors out there. Surely those smart engineers could figure it out. Unfortunately, the particular elements used in the production of blue light LEDs (which are what "white light" LEDs are made from) happen to be the most economical and efficient ones around. Switching the spectrum to be more in line with that of sunset and the incandescent bulb would impact both the cost and the efficiency, which might put a damper on sales. If they could somehow figure out a way around that, then there might be a hope for even better-quality LEDs. Until such time, here are my quality scores:

- natural daylight outside for a couple of hours during the day: 10 (best)
- natural daylight behind glass during the day: 10 (best)
- incandescent light: 10 (best)
- really good LED light: 5
- average LED light: 3 (worst)

The Cartel That Rigged the Light Bulb Game

The challenge with incandescent light bulb longevity is the Phoebus Cartel from 1924, when the manufacturers artificially shortened the lifespan of incandescent light bulbs in order to sell more of them.[6] There are a few manufacturers now coming out with "long-life incandescents" but I think a lot of innovation in this space has been curbed by the incandescent bulb being banned.

There were a lot of CFLs labeled as lasting 12,000 hours – which often didn't make it past 200 hours. Several of the tests I did are documented on the internet.[7] In this case, the most notable was a test where one CFL made it 72 hours before it died, which naturally makes one suspicious of whatever is written on the box. That said, I think that LED lights do, generally, have an authentic long lifespan.

Let's not forget the Centennial Light Bulb in Livermore, California, which has been burning for more than a million hours. That is an incandescent bulb.

6 permies.com/t/11452 (Phoebus Cartel)
7 permies.com/t/5761 (CFL longevity)

While the playing board is currently riddled with a lot of nefarious cheating, I think it's possible that we can see both LED and incandescent bulbs built in such a way that they last twenty years or more – so I think the actual longevity race is a wash.

It Says "Eco" on the Label – They Forgot to Mention "Carcinogenic"

The story on incandescent light is pretty straightforward. There isn't much to those bulbs, so while I think there is some toxicity in the manufacture and disposal, it is pretty small. And it has a magnificent track record while in use.

Let's explore the LED in comparison. Rather than the simple filament of an incandescent, an LED bulb needs a driver circuit, an LED panel, and a heat sink so that the whole thing doesn't catch on fire. The LED bulb could be a hundred times more sophisticated. And it has far more diversity in materials…highly toxic materials. A study by UC Irvine showed that LEDs are loaded with lead, arsenic, and other toxins that cause a variety of ailments, with cancer leading the parade.[8]

I need to drag out the CFL corpse again for a moment. Hundreds of CFL factory employees have needed hospitalization due to succumbing to toxins in the environment of the factories. It is recognized that CFL disposal is so toxic that there is a special disposal protocol which most people don't follow. During their use, CFLs reduce IQ, cause cancer, and can catch on fire.[9] CFL manufacturers claimed that these issues had been resolved, only it turns out they had not. These are the people who are building LED light bulbs now. I am going to speculate that LED lights will have about one third the toxic nightmare of CFLs, but they still have about twelve times more toxicity than incandescent lights. And I am going to further speculate that the same can be said for the disposal.

As for health issues for LED lights during their use, LEDs are still relatively new. So far, LED light has been proven to mess with sleep cycles. It has also shown the potential to cause problems for people with epilepsy as well as contribute to malaise, headaches, and visual impairment.[10] And apparently infrared light, which LEDs produce almost none of, is extremely important for all sorts of biological functions such as eye health and cellular energy production.[11] And those are just the problems we've figured out so far!

Quick note: If you are off-grid and you have DC power, then the electronics for LED are simpler and thus the toxicity for production and disposal is less.

If you wish to compare LED to CFL, LED is much better. But if you wish to compare the toxicity of LED to incandescent:

- Natural daylight: 10 (best)
- Natural daylight behind glass: 9.5
- Incandescent light: 9
- DC LED light: 5
- AC LED light: 1.5 (worst)

8 permies.com/t/102282 (LED toxicity)
9 permies.com/t/5759 (CFL toxicity)
10 permies.com/p/848566 (LED usage health issues)
11 permies.com/p/848567 (LED infrared)

Big Energy Savings! (Except in Cold Climates)

In general, LEDs produce about four times more light per watt than incandescent bulbs. And, unlike CFLs, they really do produce four times more light per watt. The amount of light given off at any point in the first thirty seconds is the same as the amount of light given off at ten minutes – just like incandescent. And, unlike CFLs, the amount of light it gives off five years later is the same as when it was brand new.

BUT WAIT! I live in Montana. When it gets cold outside, the days get much shorter. When I need more light, I also happen to need more heat. And incandescent light has two big properties: high-quality light and radiant heat. Hmm…

Radiant heat, when pointed at a person, is far more efficient than

> **A Quick Science Lesson**
> There are three different types of heat transfer:
>
> 1. **Conduction** occurs when two objects are physically touching. This is the most efficient form of heat transfer. Think of food in a frying pan. The heat is being conducted from the frying pan to the food. Hold your sandwich an inch away from the frying pan and you'll be waiting a while for the grilled cheese.
>
> 2. **Radiation** is energy that travels in a directional wave. When radiation strikes an object it transfers heat to it. Think of sitting around a campfire. The front half of you may be warm but your back might be cold. That's because the air itself is cold – you are being warmed by radiant heat.
>
> 3. **Convection** is heating the air, some of which heats you. This is the least efficient type of heat transfer and is sadly the way most of our homes are heated.

convective heat – which is the most common way that people heat their home.[12] If you live in a cold climate and you are using incandescent lights willy-nilly about your house, thinking only of light without a thought in the world of using them in an intelligent way, then the electricity is effectively free in the winter. The electricity is free because if you turn all of your lights off, your thermostat will then tell your heater to come on more. It will be almost exactly the same amount of energy.

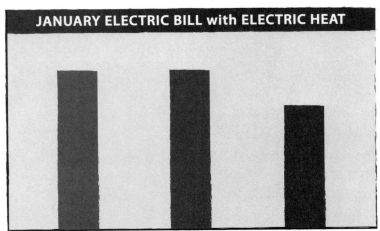

JANUARY ELECTRIC BILL with ELECTRIC HEAT

ALL LIGHTS OFF   ALL LIGHTS ON   STRATEGIC USE OF INCANDESCENT LIGHTS

12 permies.com/t/108658 (types of heat transfer)

I can do better than free. If used intelligently, the incandescent light bulb can actually REVERSE your heat bill and save HUNDREDS OF DOLLARS PER YEAR. Maybe even THOUSANDS! In 2010 I moved into a house that was heated by electric heat and, using techniques outlined in chapter 13, I cut 87% off my electric heat bill.[13] The star of the show was a 40-watt incandescent bulb. In this case, four micro heaters saved me about $900 for one winter.

So, if you live in a warm climate:

- **LED light: 10 (best)**
- **Incandescent light: 3 (worst)**

If you live in a cold climate:

- **Incandescent light used intelligently: 10 (best)**
- **Incandescent light: 5**
- **LED light: 1 (worst)**

The Ultimate Example of Greenwashing

If a person is on the grid and lives in a cold climate, there is no contest: incandescent is dramatically superior. If a person lives in a warm climate or is off-grid, they will have to wrestle with their own values to make their own choices.

The passionate armies of people fighting for CFLs and LEDs are fueled by professional greenwashing. I bought into it for a while myself. How embarrassing!

I think LEDs have come a LONG way in the last five years, and things are looking promising. I am excited about what the future might bring. And I hope that we eliminate all light bulb subsidies and artificially short product lifespans and political bans – so our future discussions can be a bit more direct.

The bottom line about light bulbs: they are too trivial to talk about in this book except to unravel the greenwashing that is preventing people from contemplating real solutions.

I'm glad we had this chat and got that out of the way. Now for the really big stuff!

13 permies.com/t/8388 (87% savings)

Chapter 4
Carbon Footprint

Most people reading this book are seriously concerned about carbon footprint. The theory, in a nutshell, is that human-generated, carbon-based emissions are creating a greenhouse effect that will warm the Earth to the point where it will no longer be able to sustain life, especially human life, and that at a particular point there will be nothing we can do to stop it. Damn. Well, I guess the good news is that when all the people are dead there will be no more war, famine, or rude internet comments either.

Of course, there are some people who do not subscribe to the carbon footprint theory. If you are one of those people, I think there are still some really awesome things in this book that will solve other problems and also keep more money in your wallet. And, if that's not enough, if you get tired of people shaking their fists at you, you can always give them a copy of this book and tell them they can't criticize you until they've taken all of the steps laid out in this book. That should get them off your back for a while.

The carbon footprint concern was presented to the masses over ten years ago by Al Gore in the movie *An Inconvenient Truth*.[1] A year later, Derrick Jensen responded with the book *As the World Burns: 50 Simple Things You Can Do to Stay in Denial*[2] and stated:

> "*An Inconvenient Truth* helped raise consciousness about global warming. But did you notice that all of the solutions presented had to do with personal consumption – changing light bulbs, inflating tires, driving half as much… Even if every person in the United States did everything the movie suggested, U.S. carbon emissions would fall by only 22 percent. Scientific consensus is that emissions must be reduced by at least 75 percent worldwide."

Jensen later points out that our total global carbon footprint is growing by 2% each year. He suggests that therefore there is no point in even trying – we would only be postponing the inevitable.

Jensen's book goes into solutions beyond being angry that are well outside my comfort zone, but, damn, that is some first-class math. I wish to crawl into the math and take a good, hard look at that 22%.

1 permies.com/t/gore
2 permies.com/t/51516 (Jensen's book)

The average annual carbon emissions per adult in the United States is somewhere around 30 tons. What bugs me about current carbon footprint "solutions" is that they are generally weak or are connected to some product for sale. It seems like most of the solutions you hear about will bring your footprint down to 29.98 tons. If we use Jensen's math, if every person were to follow every solution presented in *An Inconvenient Truth*, we would only reduce our average footprint down to 23.4 tons. And we need to get to 7.5 tons – or less!

For the record, the following are the concrete suggestions made by *An Inconvenient Truth* as viewed in 2018. All suggestions focusing directly on political action have been removed so that the list that is left is purely about what you can do personally. When I first saw the movie years ago, the thing that was buzzing through my head was that the solutions seemed very weak. I wish to complain endlessly about this list, but I will keep it brief in the interest of getting on with the book:

1. **Waste money on "energy-saving" appliances:** (Al said "Buy energy efficient appliances and light bulbs.") This sounds like a great opportunity for appliance companies to make gobs of money getting you to throw out your old, but still functional, appliances. Using a clothesline[3] and washing your clothes with cold water will save you far more energy than upgrading all of your appliances.

2. **Be colder in winter:** (Al said "Change your thermostat to reduce energy for heating & cooling.") It isn't clear if Al is suggesting buying a fancy thermostat or if he is simply suggesting that if you give up some comfort it will make a difference. On this point, Al is really onto something, but these implementations result in smaller energy savings than you might expect. You might think that this will save 10% to 15% on your total heating bill – but chances are it probably won't even be half of that.

3. **Open your door to the shenanigans of wicked light bulb companies:** (Al said "Weatherize your house, increase insulation, [and] get an energy audit.") The payback on insulation is always good – so again, a good focus on the big energy pig: heat. Unfortunately, an energy audit often just ends up making someone else more money by pushing light bulbs on you and doesn't result in real energy savings.

4. **Recycle:** This is very level 1. See chapter 8 on moving way beyond recycling for how we can significantly reduce our waste.

5. **If you can, buy a hybrid car. When you can, walk, or ride a bicycle. Where you can, use light rail and mass transit:** I like this one a lot, although I want to take it about ten times further while not giving up the freedom that comes with having your own car. When choosing a vehicle, I think electric is a good choice. There is still so much room to optimize electric vehicles, but petroleum cars are about as optimized as they are going to get. And while buying a hybrid (or fully electric) car is a good step, it is interesting to note that if you have a huge truck but only drive it once a month, you will use less fuel than someone who drives a hybrid every day. So rather than focusing so much on what you are driving, I think it is better to focus on sharing a car, getting a job that doesn't require a car, or living in a place where you don't need (or want) a car.

6. **Give your money to greenwashing:** (Al said "Switch to renewable sources of energy.") Not all sources of energy production are equal, but at the same time, renewable energy sources are not all that they are cracked up to be either. They are all flawed. We'll talk more about this in chapter 23. In short, I think that while solar is better than coal, we would be much better off if we first reduced our energy consumption by 95% and then explored the best source for our reduced needs. Coincidentally, this approach can also save thousands of dollars. Sweet.

7. **Plant trees, lots of trees:** This is a good one. Thanks, Al.

I agree with Jensen's analysis – that list was far too weak. Even when I first saw the movie, I could think of some things that would make a much stronger impact. And, today, I KNOW of dozens of things that would have far more impact. In fact, we can not only reach the 7.5 tons that Jensen points out, but the solutions presented in this book can take us to 0 tons, or negative 30 tons, or even negative 150 tons – depending on how much effort one person wants to put into this. Yes, I believe that we can have a net positive effect on the planet. All in our backyards, and all without being angry at the bad guys.[4]

Some people like to point out that "industry" emits far more greenhouse gases than individuals, and thus we are totally off the hook from doing anything about "the atrocities committed by those people." I think that the first step in changing our carbon footprint is to take ownership of our emissions and recognize that if our actions cause pollution elsewhere, those are our emissions too. Roads, public buildings, companies producing products for us, and a lot of other things are all our responsibility too. We will talk a lot more in this book about how to reduce various aspects of carbon footprint, but here are just a few to get started:

For folks living in a cold climate, heat is 55% to 75% of home energy use.[5] That would be approximately 10% of overall emissions. In chapter 13, I will introduce techniques that make a big difference – including using a rocket mass heater which you can build in a weekend for under $200 that will heat your home with the sticks that fall off the trees in your yard.[6] To put that into perspective, switching from electric heat to a rocket mass heater can have the same effect on carbon emissions as parking seven cars![7]

Taking all of the many indirect emissions into account, as crazy as it might seem, growing our own food would reduce our greenhouse gas emissions by roughly 35%.[8] On top of that, using techniques outlined in chapter 17, it is actually possible to grow food in a way that sequesters carbon instead of emitting it, so the savings would likely be quite a bit more than 35%. That's right, this one solution alone would save more carbon than all of the solutions from *An Inconvenient Truth* combined!

And we're just getting started…

4 permies.com/t/51417 (personal vs political change)
5 permies.com/p/102770 (energy breakdown)
6 permies.com/t/1078 (rocket mass heater)
7 permies.com/t/43271 (rocket mass heater emissions)
8 permies.com/t/90863 (food footprint)

Chapter 5
Petroleum Footprint

I heard about somebody making a 1500-mile (~2500 km) journey to protest oil pipeline stuff…in a sports utility vehicle…alone (read: no carpool). That's about 150 gallons (~600 liters) of fuel for the round trip. For this person, it seems that their actions say something different than their protests. I visited with about a dozen other people who made the journey to this same protest – but none of them burned through 150 gallons of petroleum to protest against petroleum.

I'm glad that people protest. It's a critical part of how we get things to work out for the best. At the same time, I wonder if their time would be better spent demonstrating lifestyles that reduce their petroleum footprint, followed by telling the world about those lifestyles.[1]

(Shhh…sneaking in a political note. Did you know that the unsubsidized price for a gallon of fuel would be more than three times higher?[2] I think that if we got rid of the oil subsidies, this problem would end instantly.)

If oil consumption can be reduced by even 10% across the board, then the effort going into building a new pipeline would fall into the space of "not worth it" and the companies would drop it.

Petroleum is used in many ways – such as producing plastic, pesticides, and fertilizer – but roughly 70% of petroleum is used for transportation. While there are a number of suggestions in this book for reducing the presence of petroleum products in your life, this chapter is going to focus primarily on petroleum used for transportation.

As with many things in this book, it would be impossible to provide an exact recipe for reducing petroleum use because every person comes from a different situation. For the sake of getting some ideas across that could have a solid impact on our petroleum footprint, I am going to simplify this whole discussion by suggesting a scenario that is extremely close to the US average…

Rudy lives in a house by himself and has exactly one car. Rudy uses 1000 gallons (~3800 liters) of fuel each year. 500 gallons (~1900 liters)

1 permies.com/t/petroleum
2 permies.com/t/108694 (fuel subsidies)

go directly into his car and the other 500 gallons are indirect – from the stuff he buys. Mostly food. Rudy commutes to work each day, 25 minutes each way (the US average).

The following are some commonly offered solutions that you are probably already familiar with:

- **Taking exceptionally good care of your car:**[3] This is, unfortunately, by far, the most common suggestion for reducing fuel consumption. Perfect tire pressure, a well-tuned engine, clean air filters, etc., might save Rudy **25 gallons (~95 liters) per year**.

- **Hypermiling:**[4] Hypermiling is a collection of techniques that help folks get better mileage with their existing vehicle. Things like driving slower, accelerating slower, gentler braking, and maybe even some small modifications to your vehicle. If Rudy does a little of this, he might save **20 gallons (~75 liters) per year**. If he is super passionate about it, he might save **100 gallons (~380 liters) per year**. If he gets to the top 1% of all people trying this, he might even save **180 gallons (~680 liters) per year**.

- **Telecommuting twice a week:**[5] **140 gallons (~530 liters) per year**.

- **Reduce commute time:** If Rudy commutes 5 minutes each way instead of 25 but still drives everywhere else, he might save **250 gallons (~950 liters) per year**. Special note: Although this does save petroleum, most of the pollution associated with driving comes within the first 5 minutes of driving while you wait for the catalytic converter to kick in – so this doesn't cut as much pollution as you might expect.

- **Get a car with better mileage:**[6] Switching from his thoroughly average car (25.5 mpg) to a Prius (50 mpg) would save Rudy **250 gallons (~950 liters) per year**.

- **Telecommuting full time: 350 gallons (~1300 liters) per year.**

- **Have no car and use public transportation: 450 gallons (~1700 liters) per year.**

- **Walk or bike everywhere or get an electric car:**[7] Rudy saves **500 gallons (~1900 liters) per year**. That's HALF! – but only half.

I think that, for a lot of people, most of these ideas sound like living a less luxuriant life. Some people might even use the word 'sacrifice.' While these things will make an impact, *we* are looking for solutions that both solve problems and allow us to live a more luxuriant life. We can do better!

The following are some solutions you may not have considered that I think can have a huge impact:

- **Sharing a home:**[8] (Assuming Rudy still commutes) People just don't need as much stuff. Even food can be purchased collectively. The reduction of overall stuff and food transportation costs saves Rudy a total of **150 gallons (~570 liters) per year**. Note that these savings are right up there with being a superstar at hypermiling. And while this may sound like a heart-wrenching

3 permies.com/t/79311 (tweaking mileage)
4 permies.com/t/hypermiling
5 permies.com/t/telecommuting
6 permies.com/t/79310 (efficient cars)
7 permies.com/t/53478 (electric cars)
8 permies.com/t/2898 (sharing a home)

sacrifice featuring a slow death by a thousand petty dramas, I will address that problem later in this book.

- **Gardening:** Rudy uses 500 gallons (~1900 liters) of petroleum per year for food. 200 gallons (~760 liters) is to fetch the food (direct), and 300 gallons (~1100 liters) is to produce, package, and transport the food to within Rudy's fetching distance (indirect). Growing a really great garden and meeting half of his total food needs saves Rudy **250 gallons (~950 liters) per year.** An utterly massive garden that meets 90% of his own food needs, and manages to provide 10% of the food needs of ten neighbors, saves **950 gallons (~3600 liters) per year.** With acreage, Rudy might grow enough food to feed five people year-round and thus save **2500 gallons (~9500 liters) per year.** That's right, he would effectively use negative amounts of petroleum by reducing someone else's footprint! To some people this might sound like a lot of work, but in chapter 17 I'll talk about growing twice the food for one tenth the effort.

- **Telecommuting from a place where a group of people share resources and a gigantic garden:** This is an attempt to paint a best-case scenario for petroleum footprint. This is a very large food system that is cared for by twenty people sharing resources on a large property. There are three cars shared by the group. Rudy finds himself driving somewhere about once a month – not because he is trying to reduce his footprint or make sacrifices for the greater good, but because he has a full, rich, and wonderful life where he is and he rarely wants to drive anywhere. Nearly all the food he eats comes from the property, and the property feeds another 100 people year round. Rudy's portion of the group's savings: **3000 gallons (~11,000 liters) per year!** That's the footprint of three people, and that's just Rudy's portion!

It might not be entirely true, but I think there is a whole lot of truth to it when Geoff Lawton[9] says:

"All the world's problems can be solved in a garden."

9 permies.com/f/152 (forum about Geoff Lawton)

Chapter 6
Toxic Footprint

People are getting sick at an alarming rate. One in three women and one in two men in America will get cancer in their lives. That's crazy! This should be a concern of epic proportions, but for some reason, most people in America seem to believe in what Joel Salatin[1] calls "the cancer fairy." During the night, the cancer fairy sits down, rolls dice, flips a coin, throws darts at a dartboard, and finally picks names out of a hat for who will be given cancer that night. Luck of the draw. Damn. Sucks to be you.

I think that cancer does not come from the cancer fairy. I think that cancer comes from carcinogens. All day, every day, people are soaking in an ocean of carcinogens. The number of toxins in homes, workplaces, vehicles, and food is staggering. And there's a pretty huge list of things currently labeled as "likely carcinogens." The worst of it is, I think that most of the toxins have not even been identified yet.

I think the way to prevent cancer and many other diseases is very simple: reduce toxins. Reduce toxins a lot. To tackle this, I wish to express that some things will have a more significant impact than others. And I want to make a list of these things, expressing how significant an impact there will be. I need units of toxicity – but this area is far too complicated for a simple metric. Therefore, to convey my point, I wish to introduce a bit of fiction to this nonfiction book. In keeping with the spirit of the cancer fairy, I hereby declare that 100 pounds of Toxic Fairy Dust (TFD) is the exact amount that will kill one standard-issue adult human.

The following are some commonly-believed sources of TFD that you are probably already familiar with:

- **Tobacco: 35 pounds TFD.**

- **Sugar:** A critical component to a magnificent huckleberry pie. And a conspirator in half of all ailments. We take sugar cane (a type of grass), smash the juice out of it and boil the water out of the juice, leaving a crusty, dried, brown scum that we crush and bleach. Your tongue's drug of choice. But I don't think we are designed to eat grass. I'm going to say that eliminating sugar may save **10 pounds TFD.**

- **High-fructose corn syrup (HFCS):[2] 20 pounds TFD.**

---

1 permies.com/t/3636 (Joel Salatin)
2 permies.com/t/hfcs

- Plastic bottles with BPAs (a well researched toxin): 10 pounds TFD.

The following are some further contributors that I think need a quick mention:

- Aspartame:[3] 30 pounds TFD.
- Sucralose: 25 pounds TFD.
- Saccharin: 3 pounds TFD.

The following are some steps I believe can have a huge impact:[4]

- Go pooless:[5] Going without soap or shampoo in the shower saves **5 pounds TFD**. More about this in chapter 15.

- Stop drinking and bathing in poison: Chlorine is straight-up poison. It kills all living things. Cities are required to chlorinate water. If you drink it, the idea is that the chlorine is significant enough to kill most of the organisms in the water, but not enough to kill you. Eliminating poison in your water supply saves **5 pounds TFD**.

- Stop using teflon[6] and plastic containers: Eliminating nasty stuff from coming into contact with our food once we bring it inside saves **10 pounds TFD**. More about this in chapter 15.

- Stop eating food loaded with toxins: Eating healthy polyculture-grown food from a garden instead of food loaded with insecticides, herbicides, fungicides, hormones, antibiotics, and other toxic gick saves **35 pounds TFD**. Lots more about this later in the book.

- Eliminate 98% of household cleaners: The stuff they put in household cleaners is incredibly dangerous. It's also mostly unnecessary. Replacing commercial cleaners with edible cleaners or hot water saves **45 pounds TFD**.[7] More about this in chapter 15.

- Live in a house made of toxin-free materials:[8] The materials used in constructing modern homes are full of off-gassing toxins. There are so many toxins in a standard new home that if the air in the house is not exchanged with fresh outside air every few hours, you may die! Living in a home that is at least six years old and has had a chance to off-gas may save **25 pounds TFD** when compared to the first month living in a brand new home. Living in a house built entirely of natural materials will save another **5 pounds TFD**.

- Avoid the big brown cloud: When I did the commuter job many years ago, I remember being able to see the huge brown cloud over the city and thinking about how I could not get away from breathing that. Even now, when I visit a city, it just stinks of a constant barrage of vehicle exhaust. Then there's the random whiff of some chemical I cannot identify, followed by the odor of tobacco enhanced with perfumes. And is it just me, or are there a lot of pest

3 permies.com/t/aspartame
4 permies.com/t/108697 (reducing toxins)
5 permies.com/t/pooless
6 permies.com/t/teflon
7 permies.com/t/107215 (edible cleaners)
8 permies.com/t/88283 (toxin-free house materials)

control vehicles? The big, brown cloud is a soup made of many wastes of many colors. Outside of the city, there can be challenges if you live near property that has a different cloud of some sort. But there are places that are remote from any of those clouds. **20 pounds TFD**.

Once we have reduced the toxins in our environment by a significant extent, the majority of illnesses may just disappear. To better understand this topic, I wish to direct you to three documentaries:

- *The Food Cure:*[9] Six people beat cancer by eliminating toxins from their personal environment.

- *Chemerical:*[10] A family switches from conventional cleaners to organic. By the end of the movie, not only is the entire family healthier, but the mother appears to have gained 30 IQ points.

- *Stink:*[11] After cancer takes a mother, the father explores the toxicity of everyday products - with a focus on a pair of pajamas for a daughter.

Reducing the toxins in our environment is a subject big enough to fill a library with books. There are always new "nontoxic" solutions being offered, some of which are authentically nontoxic and most of which will hide their true toxicity for decades. It's complicated. It also doesn't have to be complicated. Similar to the other problems already presented and the many problems unnamed, the solutions and strategies presented in this book would go a long way toward a healthier, happier, more luxuriant life for people on a sustainable Earth.

9 permies.com/t/32423 (*The Food Cure*)
10 permies.com/t/chemerical
11 permies.com/t/stink

Part 2
General Strategies

Chapter 7
The Wheaton Eco Scale

Ten years ago, a newspaper columnist quit her "trying to be green" column after one year. Readers would write in, telling her what to put in the column. Eventually, those messages came with the words "or else." She decided to end the column after receiving death threats from several readers. Readers that are all about hearts, flowers, and rainbows…and, apparently, death threats.

To respond to this travesty, I created the Wheaton Eco Scale.[1] Since its creation, this scale has been handy for hundreds of things. Every person who reads this book will be at a different point on the journey toward ecological awesomeness. Talking to others about their journey can be inspiring, humbling, annoying, or infuriating. My hope is that this scale will reduce conflict and improve acceptance in the struggle for solving global problems. I encourage you to make up scales too. It's fun!

I went to the scale store and decided that I wanted the very best for you. So I selected a "base-10 reverse logarithmic scale." Yummy. Here is how it turned out:

At level 0 there are about 6 billion people (about 80% of the population).

At level 1 there are 1 billion people (about 15% of the population).

At level 2 there are 100 million people (about 1.5% of the population).

At level 3 there are 10 million people (about 0.15% of the population).

At level 4 there are 1 million people.

At level 5 there are 100,000 people.

At level 6 there are 10,000 people.

At level 7 there are 1,000 people.

At level 8 there are 100 people.

At level 9 there are 10 people.

At level 10 there is 1 person.

Before giving you an idea of what might place you at a particular level, I wish to first share two critical observations about this scale:

1 permies.com/t/scale

The first observation is that most people find folks one or two levels above them to be pretty cool. But people three levels up seem a bit nutty. People four or five levels up seem downright crazy. And people six levels up should probably be institutionalized "for their own safety and the safety of those around them." I find the latter reactions to be inappropriate. If people seem crazy, they might just be advanced on the same path you're following.

The second observation is that most people find folks one level back to be ignorant, and people two levels back seem like assholes. Any further back and people start to think that the person should be shot on sight for the betterment of society as a whole. I find that *all* of these reactions are inappropriate – people will not change if you yell at them or hit them with sticks. But they *will* change if you tell them about the cool stuff that's just a little bit ahead of where they are now and skip the stuff that is far ahead of them.

Below are some possible attributes of people on the Wheaton Eco Scale. Keep in mind that this is not a checklist or a quiz meant to place you at a particular level, but an effort to paint a general picture of what the different levels look like. If you don't know what something means, don't worry, we've got lots of book left.

> **Level 0:** Thinking about the environment is something that "other people" do. If a level 0 person sees a dandelion in their yard, their solution is poison. Average carbon footprint of 30 tons.

> **Level 1:** Thinking about the environment. Bought some "better" light bulbs.[2] Trying some recycling. Reads an article or two. Buys some organic food. Their power bill is less than average.[3] Learning how to compost. Carbon footprint is 29 tons.

> **Level 2:** Has a recycling system. Reads at least one article a week. Power bill is 80% of average. 30% of purchased food is organic. 10% of purchased food is local.[4] Growing a small garden. Has a compost pile. Learning about natural building.[5] Has attended some free workshops and lectures. Maybe read a book. Pulls dandelions. Carbon footprint is 27 tons.

> **Level 3:** Contemplating "zero waste"[6] and producing about a tenth of the landfill material of an average person. Has a pretty good-sized organic garden – grows about 20% of their own food. 80% of purchased food is organic. 2% of food is wildcrafted. Power bill is half of the average. Reads something almost every day. Has read a few things about permaculture. Has read at least a couple dozen books.[7] Has attended several paid workshops. Pooless.[8] No more fluorescent light bulbs.[9] Avid composter. Has eliminated 95% of the toxic gick from their home.[10] Very concerned about environmental problems. Carbon footprint is 20 tons.

> **Level 4:** Grows 50% of their own food. 95% of purchased food is organic. 8% of food is wildcrafted. Passionately studying permaculture. Incandescent lights are

2 permies.com/t/led
3 permies.com/t/conservation
4 permies.com/t/3679 (local vs organic)
5 permies.com/t/1611 (wofati eco building)
6 permies.com/t/107888 (zero waste)
7 permies.com/t/31762 (100+ book reviews)
8 permies.com/t/pooless
9 richsoil.com/cfl
10 permies.com/t/108697 (reducing toxins)

preferred and used wisely. Power bill is 30% of average. Allows dandelions, eats some of them, and enjoys blowing on dandelion seed heads.[11] Carbon footprint is 10 tons.

Level 5: Has taken a permaculture design course (PDC).[12] Grows 90% of their own food. Participating in building/sharing knowledge online. Might teach a small free class or workshop. Carbon footprint is zero.

Level 6: Living a footprint that is one tenth of the average. Maybe living in community.[13] Maybe living in something very small.[14] Actively sharing knowledge and starting to get paid to teach. Exchanges dandelion seeds with others to get a really great tasting dandelion. Carbon footprint is -30 tons.

Level 7: Teaching PDCs. Inventing things that will change our future for the better. Writing a first book or creating a first movie that will influence the future. Influencing thousands of people to make significant changes for the better. Carbon footprint is -200 tons.

Level 8: Writing many books, creating many movies – influencing millions of people to make significant changes for the better. Doing things that are improving the world in big ways. Carbon footprint is -1000 tons.

Level 9: Willie Smits,[15] Masanobu Fukuoka,[16] Paul Stamets,[17] Art Ludwig,[18] Bill Mollison,[19] Ianto Evans,[20]...

Level 10: Sepp Holzer [21]

It's my scale, so I can put whomever I want at level 10. I choose Sepp Holzer. If you want someone else at level 10, go make your own scale.

I wish to reiterate that my mission with this scale is **NOT** to assign everybody a number. My mission is to clarify a problem. The real point I needed to make was about how people who are on the eco path tend to despise the people behind them and think the people way ahead of them are nuts. I have seen this happen hundreds of times. I hope that by showing the scale, people will be more aware of the problem and, hopefully, we will have better progress.

11 permies.com/t/dandelion
12 permies.com/t/19679 (podcast about PDCs)
13 permies.com/t/community
14 permies.com/t/1765 (house size)
15 permies.com/t/8596 (Willie Smits)
16 permies.com/t/2214 (Masanobu Fukuoka)
17 permies.com/t/41900 (Paul Stamets)
18 permies.com/t/43124 (Art Ludwig)
19 permies.com/t/59144 (Bill Mollison)
20 permies.com/t/44429 (Ianto Evans)
21 richsoil.com/sepp

Chapter 8
Moving Way Beyond
Recycling

Recycling has been around for a long time.[1] Depending on how you define "recycling," maybe forever. Nature is an expert recycler. There is no such thing as waste in a natural system. If nature was not so good at recycling, we'd be standing atop a mountain of dead trees, dead bodies, and a slime mountain made of expired bacteria that just never got taken care of. For most of living history, humanity's waste footprint on the Earth was basically non-existent.[2] Then we learned how to do things with oil like creating plastic and styrofoam and a whole bunch of other "convenient" and "modern" things that, coincidentally, take a really, really long time to break down.

The mountains of garbage that we have been piling up over the last hundred years are turning into environmental disasters beyond something we can ever repair. Recycling was our first attempt to mitigate this problem. This system has evolved over the years and has reduced our garbage problems. But wait! At the same time, we have increased the amount of garbage that the average adult produces. And a lot of our recycling paths are breaking down because they are overloaded. Some of it just gets put into landfills anyway. So, we are recycling now, but the problems are even worse!

Attack of the Pizza Box

Somebody asked on the internet "What should I do with pizza boxes? Because there is food on the cardboard, we are not allowed to recycle it."

The answer with the most likes frustrated me. I felt they were taking one problem and converting it to a different problem: using the cardboard as mulch in a garden. The problem with this is that the paper in the cardboard is loaded with toxic gick.[3] But, clearly, most people are not aware of this.

The next most popular answer was a 100% solution: stop having pizza delivered. But on the downside, I very much wish for people to live a far more luxuriant life while making the world a better place – not sacrificing the small things that bring joy. I think that rather than the short answer of "don't" let's instead consider a life so luxuriant that we don't even want pizza delivered anymore. For example, if there happens to be a person in our house who

1 permies.com/t/recycling
2 permies.com/t/8382 (waste history)
3 permies.com/t/2157 (toxic cardboard)

regularly makes amazing pizza from scratch, then I suspect the desire for delivered pizza becomes moot.

Since most people reading something like this on the internet will not accept an answer that doesn't fit into a bumper sticker, we move on to what I think was the best bumper sticker answer: use the cardboard as a fire starter. This was sadly the least liked answer. I wish it had many more likes and also said "for a rocket mass heater" – which would also eliminate any smoky pollution that would result from burning the cardboard somewhere else. We'll talk more about rocket mass heaters and their incredible efficiency in chapter 13.

Recycling 2.0, 3.0, 4.0, and 5.0

Most recycling systems are composed of 3 bins: a black bin for "garbage," a blue bin for "recyclables," and a green bin for "compostables."

Let's start by saying that a person in Eco Level 0 puts absolutely everything in the black bin – if they are allowed to. For example's sake, let's say they put in 100 units of waste.

Think of this as a game. We want to have the lowest score in town. A unit of waste in the blue or green bins counts as 1 point. A unit of waste in the black bin counts as 4 points. So the maximum possible score is **400 points.**

The folks at Eco Level 1 will be trying some recycling. They might reduce the amount of waste going into the black bin by half, and they will redirect the waste into the blue and green bins. Let's say 50 units in the black bin, 30 units in the blue bin, and 20 units in the green bin. **250 points.**

A person at Eco Level 2 will take it up a notch. Reduce, reuse, repair, recycle is a list of things they do in order. They begin repairing old clothing[4] and tools.[5] They buy some things at the thrift store. They hold a yard sale and attend numerous others. They make conscious buying decisions to have more durable products and lower package waste.[6] They realize that homemade meals are far more enjoyable than highly processed packaged "meals" from the store.[7] They significantly reduce the number of plastic beverage bottles in their house. Paper or cardboard is used as fire starter in the winter time, saving a bunch of work chopping kindling.[8] 25 units go in the black bin, 15 units in the blue bin, and 10 units in the green bin. **125 points.**

At Eco Level 3, a person is starting to grow their own food, reducing the amount of food packaging in their house further. They have implemented reuse and repair such that they don't buy nearly as much stuff anymore.[9, 10] They have eliminated plastic water bottles by 95% or more. They have set up a free shed in their neighborhood where one person's junk can become another person's treasure. They have reduced the amount of cheap electronics they buy, opting instead for devices that will last longer. They have also realized that the compost they have been getting from the town's composting service is filled

4 permies.com/t/54406 (mending clothes)
5 permies.com/t/61057 (tool maintenance)
6 permies.com/t/86764 (life without plastic)
7 permies.com/t/48146 (cheap homemade meals)
8 permies.com/t/77432 (fire starter)
9 permies.com/t/38176 (reuse art)
10 permies.com/t/12412 (reuse projects)

with toxins[11] and so decide to make their own compost instead of using the green bin. Now they have 12 units in the black bin and 12 units in the blue bin. **60 points.**

At Eco Level 4, a person is growing 50% of their own food, really cutting down on food packaging. This person may live in community with a bunch of other people, reducing the amount of things being purchased by a significant factor.[12] They are exploring doing their own glass recycling using a Fresnel lens or in the core of a rocket mass heater.[13] They might even recycle their neighbor's glass for them since they can make money from it. They are now putting 6 units in the black bin and 6 units in the blue bin. **30 points.**

Growing 90% of their own food, people at Eco Level 5 have nearly eliminated food packaging. They have eliminated most of the household products that aren't really needed. Most of their furniture and tools are handcrafted out of natural materials. They occasionally treat themselves to a bag of chips or a tub of ice cream, but otherwise they are content to live the permaculture dream. They now put 3 units in the black bin and 3 units in the blue bin. They get their bins picked up once a year. **15 points.**

By the time someone reaches Eco Level 5 they will have reduced their total waste by 94%, drastically reducing pollution in the landscape. Beyond level 5, things get even better.

11 permies.com/t/57773 (toxic compost)
12 permies.com/t/community
13 permies.com/t/85166 (glass recycling)

Chapter 9
Vote with
Your Wallet

If we take the food away from the monster it will shrivel up and die. At the same time, people protest fracking from their home that is heated and powered by fracking. Or protest chem-ag with a mouthful of chem-ag food. It seems silly to protest a monster's actions while simultaneously giving that monster enormous amounts of money. Once this conflict is pointed out, most people give up on their quest because they don't see an obvious, simple, and fast solution. Or they think that all of the solutions stink of frustrating sacrifice.

The problem is not that there are no good alternative solutions to vote for, it's that oftentimes, people don't know that any good solutions exist. It would not be in the fracking companies' best interests to convince you to use less natural gas. So unless you go digging for solutions yourself, you're not going to hear about good ways to cut your natural gas usage. The only reason farmers are currently doing conventional ag is because they've only been presented with the fancy brochures on chem-ag by the chem-ag companies. Since there is no massive middle person in permaculture, there is no one sending farmers the brochures on permaculture that tell them they don't need chem-ag to feed the world or turn a profit. Please allow me to offer alternative candidates when it comes to voting with your wallet. Candidates that provide a more luxuriant life at less expense while embracing our values.

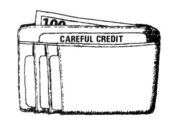

Natural gas is America's favorite form of heat, and it is now getting quite popular for generating electricity too. If you allow yourself only six seconds to solve the problem of fracking for natural gas, you are probably stuck with being cold. Or damn cold. Or building a brand new passive solar home that is super insulated. This sounds uncomfortable or like a lot of work. In chapter 13 we will explore solutions for heating the people instead of the whole house. This can cut 50% to 90% off your heating bill… while keeping you warm. Maybe some folks will only do 50%, but, hey, that could still be hundreds of dollars a year in your pocket instead of in the fracking companies' pockets. That would go a long way in making the fracking monster go hungry. But we have more: a rocket mass heater is cheap to build and will effectively eliminate your heating costs while providing luxuriant heat. Further still – if you are going to build a house, we will talk about a better option than passive solar in chapter 30.

If you are against chem-ag toxins in your food, or if you are against your taxes being used to subsidize chem-ag,[1] then stop buying chem-ag foods. And if you are against mass deforestation and mass habitat destruction, then stop buying palm oil.[2] My hope is that someday the food at all grocery stores will be permaculture food[3] because the demand for permaculture food makes it so that all farmers make more money growing with permaculture than with other systems. It would be the result of consumers voting with their wallet. At first blush, a lot of people will be concerned that buying organic (or better) food is going to cost way more than chem-ag food. I think that in order to make this comparison fair, the long-term costs of healthcare associated with eating chem-ag foods should be factored in. As Joel Salatin[4] has said: "If you think the price of organic food is expensive, have you priced cancer lately?" That said, using techniques outlined in chapter 17, it is possible to grow some, or possibly all, of your own food for little effort and way less money than any food you can buy at the store.

For every problem that comes up, try to see if your wallet is feeding the monster. If it is, then the mission becomes "how do I stop feeding the monster and lead a more luxuriant life?" If the solution eludes you after at least five minutes of deep consideration, come ask our community,[5] and we'll figure it out together. Once you've cleaned up your own backyard (literally or figuratively), then share what you have done with others who are still upset about the problem. That's all it might take to change the world.

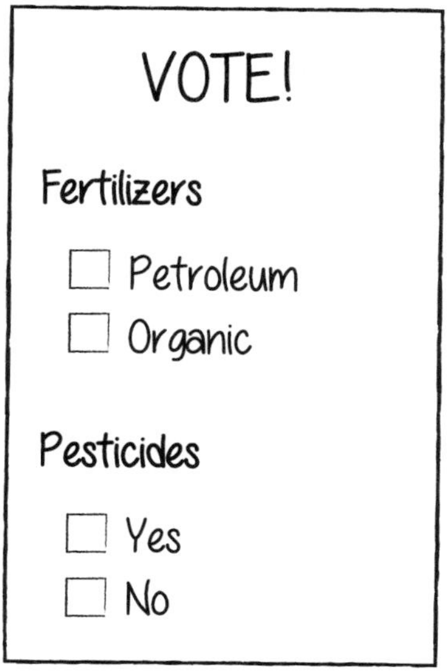

VOTE!

Fertilizers

☐ Petroleum
☐ Organic

Pesticides

☐ Yes
☐ No

1 permies.com/t/16161 (food subsidies)
2 permies.com/t/102200 (palm oil)
3 permies.com/t/56746 (permaculture groceries)
4 permies.com/t/3636 (Joel Salatin)
5 permies.com/forums

Chapter 10
Radically Deviant
Financial Strategies

You have my permission to cackle wildly if you happen to implement any of these techniques.

The Story of Gert: A Millionaire Life Without a Million Dollars

Over the decades, I have met people who live a magnificent life and have no job. I thought "Why do I have to work and they don't? They must have a trust fund or something." Nope. The answer turns out to be stupidly simple. My attempts to share what I learned were futile, until I came up with the story of Ferd and Gert.[1]

Ferd works a job for 40 hours per week. He spends about half an hour commuting each way – so that is now effectively 45 hours per week. Ferd spends 10 hours per week on feeding himself: driving to restaurants, waiting in line at restaurants, ordering, waiting…driving to grocery stores to get his favorite foods with the best price,

1 permies.com/t/gert

shopping, waiting in line, etc. After his monthly expenses, Ferd has about $200 per month of disposable income. And maybe $800 in the bank. Ferd spends nearly all of his disposable income on fun things. He is looking for entertainment and life substance. Ferd dreams of having a million dollars so that he doesn't have to work anymore. If he had a million dollars, he could buy a better house, a better car, awesome toys, and he would no longer have to work at this sucky job – or any sucky job. Ferd earns $40,000 per year now. In twenty years, he will have had several small raises such that, by the time the years have passed, he will have earned, cumulatively, a million dollars.

Gert has realized the permaculture dream. She lives on a few acres and eats the food that grows there. During the warmer months, she spends some time harvesting and preserving food. During a week or two in the fall, Gert is working a good fifty hours a week. But for most of the year, she is working less than ten hours a week. Gert also spends about ten hours a week making her meals. Usually, it is something quick, but sometimes she makes something more elaborate. Neighbors sometimes buy some of Gert's excess food. Once a year, she will help with a permaculture design for somebody. Gert has a little pickup, but she hasn't fired it up in three months. She has about $300 per month of disposable income and $4000 in the bank. Gert has trouble spending this extra money. She's not sure what to spend it on. It just sort of accumulates. Gert earns about $7000 per year now. She intends to earn less money in future years. Over the next twenty years, Gert will have earned $100,000.

If Gert had a million dollars, what would she do with it? How would her life change? Since Gert is a fictitious person in my head, I hereby declare that her life would not change. If your life does not change if you have a million dollars, then is it fair to say that you are living the life of a millionaire? Maybe we could call this being a "permaculture millionaire"?

Maybe Gert should write a book and tell the world all this. But…Gert doesn't feel like it. Gert is a humble woman and thinks nobody would want to hear that. Gert is more of a reader than a writer anyways. Plus, there are already dozens of lovely permaculture books,[2] so she doesn't feel like she needs to write another one.

Maybe Gert should get more acres and sell more food...market the food to get more per pound than what people pay at Whole Foods – maybe get $20 per pound and have five or six people move onto her land and scale up.[3] Set the pace for permaculturists all over the world! Nah, that sounds like a lot of hard work and stress.

Maybe Gert should teach some classes at her place so people can learn from her example? Gert doesn't feel like a teacher. Plus, to pull this off, she would have to do advertising and marketing, which really isn't her thing.

Maybe Gert should go onto the internet and tell the world about her lifestyle. She tried that a couple of times and was told by a few dozen people that she's a lying monster and a shill. So she decided to not bring this stuff up on the internet anymore.[4] I think the world has at least a million Gerts. Most might get an even easier life if they heard about permaculture, but they are, nonetheless, living the dream.

Not only is Gert not angry at bad guys, she doesn't even know they exist.

I am thinking of giving Ferd a million dollars. But I think telling him about Gert might be of greater value.

Owning a Home Without Grovelling to a Bank

You have my permission to make rude gestures in the general direction of any bank if you implement any of these techniques.

When hearing about Gert for the first time, the most common response is "how did she get the land?" One possible approach to achieving Gert-hood is well-documented in Rob Roy's book *Mortgage Free.*[5]

To sum up Rob's entire book in one paragraph: Keep working your day job, significantly reduce your expenses, and save up a big chunk of money. Use this money to buy your land...yes, with cash.[6] Next, build a rough shelter (basically a shack) on your land and move in. You won't have to pay rent somewhere else, so you'll have extra money to save up. While you are living in the shack, use the money you have been saving and your new shack-building skills to build a small house. Over the next number of years, keep adding on to and remodeling the house as your needs and budget allow until it becomes your dream home.

Now you have your dream home on your own land and no mortgage! Hurray! This strategy can definitely work...but living in a shack for a year doesn't really jibe with a lot of people. Fair enough. Have no fear, for those of you not interested in the shack lifestyle, we'll be introducing a luxury model at the end of the chapter.

2 permies.com/t/31762 (100+ book reviews)
3 permies.com/t/7474 (scale up)
4 permies.com/t/34441 (permaculture velocity)
5 permies.com/t/22168 (*Mortgage Free*)
6 permies.com/t/46594 (land advice)

Early Retirement Extreme

Another excellent example of how one might achieve Gert-hood is what Jacob Lund Fisker did. Once upon a time, Jacob worked as a nuclear astrophysicist. One day, he wanted to go out and play, but careers typically don't allow that on a weekday. So, rather than spend the rest of his life doing what he was trained to do, he plotted and schemed a way to escape. He ended up retiring at the age of 33 – so very clever!

Leading up to his retirement, Jacob created a blog, book, and forum called *Early Retirement Extreme* (ERE) to share his ideas and philosophies with others on how to achieve financial independence and retire early.[7] Thousands of people have shared online about their success with Jacob's strategies. In a nutshell, Jacob begs you to consider the conventional retirement path, and then consider an extreme early retirement scenario. And then consider something in between that would be best for you. Even more, you might be willing to try a path where you retire in ten years, but after a few months (perhaps after an especially comical day at work), you might be willing to try something more extreme. It seems that a lot of people who start on this path end up retiring in three years.

A quick peek at what most consider as the most extreme path: Continue working a normal job, but live so frugally that you are squirreling away 75% of your income. Try to get your living expenses under $500 per month.[8] Yes, this might seem really low but he outlines how it can be done. Invest that extra coin. When you have enough saved, you can then leave the rat race behind and spend the rest of your life in happy retirement. As a bonus, you might develop some hobbies that accidentally produce a bit more income. Oops!

Jacob is brilliant. I wish that I had learned of this when I was young. That said, while these techniques may work, the idea of living extremely frugally doesn't really seem like it fits the idea of a more luxuriant life for a lot of people. Don't worry, we'll get to a more luxuriant approach soon.

Give a Gift to Your Future Self with Passive Income Streams

The stumble I experience with Jacob's ERE is the investing part. It smells a lot like gambling to me. And since I am not a master of this type of gambling, I suspect that I will be on the losing end of the gamble while experts fleece my monies – and I am left with nothing but stabby thoughts about those experts.

Years ago, I stumbled onto "passive income streams."[9] Also called "residual income streams" or even "royalties." The idea behind passive income streams is that you put in an effort now to create something, and over the years a small trickle of money comes in without much further effort.

I wrote an article on my richsoil website about ants and aphids back in 2002.[10] It took me about two hours. I may have spent another two hours telling folks about it. This was one of my least popular articles. At some point, I stuck a couple of ads on the page and it consistently brought in about $60 per year every year. That may not sound like a lot, but it has now been 17 years, and I have made $960 from only four hours of work. That's $240 per hour! Extrapolating these figures, if you were to work 40 hours per week for a whole year doing this kind of thing, you could make $30,000

---

7 permies.com/t/ere
8 permies.com/t/93089 (living debt free)
9 permies.com/t/16439 (passive income)
10 richsoil.com/antsandaphids

per year...but after the first year, you will barely have to do anything. Sounds like a great retirement to me!

Some of my efforts in this space have never made me a dime. Some of them have needed me to foolishly spend money. Others have made me a little and a few have made me quite a bit. As with many things, I think the key is:

Try 100 things. Only 2 of them will work out, but you never know in advance which 2.[11]

One thing you can be assured of: if you do zero things, zero will work out. Here's an abbreviated list of passive income streams:[12]

- Create web pages with affiliate links[13] or ads.
- Write a book (do you like my book so far?).
    - Tip for beginners: go to some forum and write helpful answers. After a year, massage all of those answers into an ebook.
- Create a DVD-like thing (have you seen my rocket mass heater DVDs?[14]).
- Stock photography.
- Stock video.
- Be a famous movie star who gets paid in royalties.
- Be a mediocre youtube personality.
- Be a famous rock star who gets paid in royalties.
- Make music and put it up on music sites where folks can download it for a buck or two.
- Connect a perennial AdWords ad to an affiliate product.
    - Amazon pays 5% to 8%.
    - Some programs pay 20% to 80%.
- Create a massive business and hire a freakishly awesome and trustworthy person to run it (and hope it doesn't turn into an episode of *Murder She Wrote*).
- Invest money wisely[15] (note: this is what Jacob is suggesting in his ERE book).
- Make worksheets for teachers – excellent opportunities for comedy.
- Make sermons for pastors – SUPER opportunities for comedy!
- Put your drawings and art on DeviantArt.
- Make art for T-shirts and other merchandise and put them up at a site that will give you money for every shirt/thing sold.
- Find a book that you love that is self-published. Get permission from the author to make a rough audiobook (complete with a strong recommendation

11 permies.com/t/45415 (try 100 things)
12 permies.com/t/52364 (passive income ideas)
13 permies.com/t/affiliate
14 permies.com/t/63837 (RMH DVDs)
15 permies.com/t/20180 (investing)

to buy the physical book at each chapter break; especially good if the book has pictures and tables that will not convey into an audio format and the message between chapters points that out). Read the book into an mp3 file. Sell the audiobook.

- Give one thousand things away for free.[16] Videos, articles, podcasts, ebooks… it is so weird, but after a thousand it is as if you now have mystery income, good luck, money offers for stuff, and all sorts of money things that you could never have predicted before. It's a bit like magic and impossible to predict. I have to say that I have given away thousands of things with no intent of ever getting money back and, mysteriously, money has shown up in the strangest ways.

- Be creative. Come up with a dozen things not on this list.

The BEER Plan

Oh, sure, Jacob's *ERE* and Rob's *Mortgage Free* are genius. And yet I just can't leave well enough alone. I now present to you my plan that will allow you to achieve Gerthood without a lot of sacrifice involved. I call it "Better Extreme Early Retirement" (BEER). You know it is better, because the acronym spells something. And I predict more people will like it for mysterious, subliminal reasons.

The BEER plan goes as follows: Keep working your job. But for two hours every week, do something that you enjoy doing that might turn into a passive income stream. After doing this for a while, you might find that you get to a point where the amount of money you have coming in from passive income streams is greater than your monthly expenses. Since you have then effectively been earning a double income, you have saved up a lot of money. Perhaps now is the perfect time to buy your land.

Now, if you're not into the *Mortgage Free* shack approach, just keep doing what you were doing, and you'll continue to save a bunch of money. Using this money, you can go the route of building a small house on your land and then adding on to it later. Or you can keep saving up and then just build your house. Or, if you don't feel like building a house, maybe you can save up enough money to the point where you can just pay someone else to do it for you.

The endgame of the BEER plan is to have land with a home and a permaculture garden. You get there because of passive income streams. The home and the garden make it so your annual expenses drop to nearly zero. But your passive income streams keep paying. It is possible that your income becomes ten times greater than your expenses…so I guess you don't need that day job anymore.

A Clever Recipe for More Luxuriant Living at Half the Cost

The following recipe is a quick way to solve more than half of the problems we are concerned with in this book. It also reduces expenses by half or more, and, simultaneously, universally, dramatically, improves luxury.

This recipe also has an overwhelming downside. The solutions to the downside will not fit in this book. I have dedicated an enormous part of my life to trying to solve this one massive problem so that we can all harvest the magnificent benefits.

People avoid living with other people because there is just too much drama. If there was a big volume knob on drama, we could just turn it from "9" down to less than "1." What remains is that we could live with twenty other people in a far more

16 permies.com/t/18851 (giving away)

luxuriant environment.[17] And it would cost less than half as much as living alone. For starters, rent (of house or land) could be split by twenty people. Nearly any item you buy, whether it be a couch, an electric tractor, or a jigsaw puzzle, could be split by twenty people. And whenever something breaks, it's like having a 95% off coupon on repairs (and 95% of the time, the item magically repairs itself). Childcare could be shared. Food costs could be reduced through bulk ordering, and food is also more likely to get consumed before it goes bad.[18] As an example, when I lived in a household of ten where all food was shared, the cost per person per month for all-organic food (including meat) was only $108.

The benefits are profound. Community living is a magnificent, radically deviant, phenomenally effective financial strategy. Possibly for experts only until we develop better recipes to reduce drama.[19] We will explore the advantages of community living some more when we get to chapters 13 and 14.

A Few Experiments Being Conducted on Human Beings

As I am writing this, I am currently conducting four experiments that have active participants. I'll need a few years of documented results before these ideas can have a book of their own, and then they can be expanded to work on thousands of properties:

- **Ant Village:**[20] Rent a Gert-sized plot with low annual rent and strict permaculture standards.
- **Deep roots:**[21] Low lifetime rent on a Gert-sized plot.
- **The Permaculture Bootcamp:**[22] Learn permaculture through a lot of hard work in exchange for an Ant Village package or a Deep Roots package.
- **PEP:**[23] A huge list of experiences, most of which you can do at home. Document and prove your accomplishments online using your cell phone. People are looking to will their land to folks with enough experience.

17 permies.com/t/community
18 permies.com/t/6441 (community food costs)
19 permies.com/t/76639 (reducing drama)
20 permies.com/t/44793 (ant village)
21 permies.com/t/24680 (deep roots)
22 permies.com/t/bootcamp
23 permies.com/t/96687 (What is PEP?)

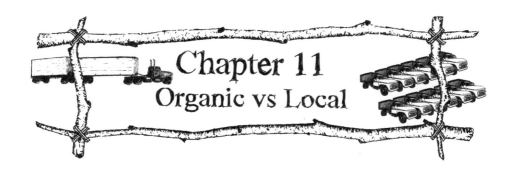

Chapter 11
Organic vs Local

My impression is that most folks wanna buy local so that there is less petroleum used. They will drive 40 minutes to the farmer or 10 minutes to the farmer's market to get food.

I think there are lots of good reasons to buy local, but I also think the whole petroleum argument doesn't work out mathematically.[1] After all, that food from 1500 miles (~2400 km) away probably went by big train, big boat, and/or big truck – filled to optimal capacity. And then the boat/train/truck was loaded with something else for the return trip. So I suspect that the transportation costs were quite optimized and, therefore, the use of petroleum per pound of food was greatly reduced for the sake of simple profit motivation.

I helped out with a farmer's market booth a few times. A big box truck was loaded to about 10% of capacity and driven to the market – about 40 miles (~65 km). About half of the produce went back for the return trip. This did not seem particularly efficient.

Now let's work in the organic component. Conventional crops will nearly always use conventional fertilizers, pesticides, etc. Nearly all of which are petroleum based. Which were processed using a lot of energy and then trucked a long way to the farm. At least 1500 miles (~2400 km). It typically takes 10 calories of petroleum to grow one calorie of conventional food.[2]

You might think you can gauge the amount of petroleum in conventional food by the price – after all, there cannot possibly be $2 worth of petroleum tied up in $1 of carrots. But most conventional foods are subsidized at least 75%.[3] Organic food is typically not subsidized.

I wonder if there might be some conventional growers who were worried about losing market to the organic folks. So I wonder if they got behind the "buy local" thing in an effort to ride that pony into town. A lot of people now have a strong preference for local over organic – and that gets my blood angered up!

1 permies.com/t/3679 (organic vs local)
2 permies.com/t/108765 (food efficiency)
3 permies.com/t/16161 (food subsidies)

Let's go back to voting with your wallet: vote for "big ag" or the little guy? Vote for petroleum fertilizers or organic? Vote for pesticides or against? If you have a local farmer who produces organic, then the choice is simple. If you have local farmers and none of them are organic, then it would seem that you desire a choice that is both local and organic. Giving your money to a non-organic farmer does NOT solve the problem. Telling these local farmers that you cannot spend your money on their wares *might* solve the problem.

When I am at the grocery store or the farmer's market, I choose to only see the organic food. And if some of it is local, I prefer that.

I hereby give:

- 1 pound of love for local (within 200 miles [~320 km] of me)

- 10 pounds of love for organic

- 100 pounds of love for organic grown within 2 miles (~3 km) of my house

- 1000 pounds of love for organic grown in my own garden

- 10,000 pounds of love for permaculture food grown in my own garden (more on this in part 4 of this book)

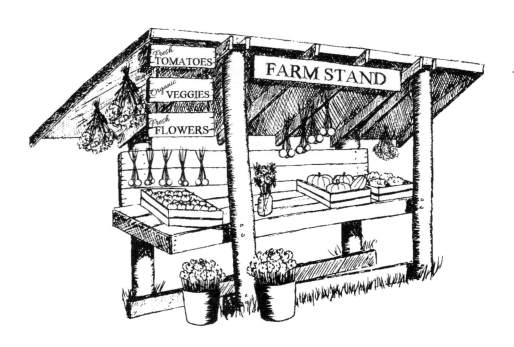

Chapter 12
Vegan vs Omnivore
vs Junk Food

I want to start by saying that I think travelling the vegan path is a noble thing: sacrificing bacon, cheese, ice cream, honey, steak…and even sacrificing a traditional Thanksgiving turkey dinner for the sake of others. Often "others" would include animals. Thanks, vegans – you folks are super cool.

I feel like I share the values of vegans, and, as bizarre as it sounds, I choose to continue to eat some meat and animal products. I have a rich buffet of thoughts, feelings, experiences, and history with this topic. By sharing some of my crazy, maybe the vegan and omnivore camps can be brought a bit closer, maybe the labels will prove insufficient, and maybe a few people will switch camps.

Many vegans point to the problems with Concentrated Animal Feed Operations (CAFOs) – and I agree with their argument against CAFOs. A literal "toxic shit storm." I am choosing to skip the gruesome details. That said, I am of the opinion that caring for animals in a way analogous to their nature is an excellent way to heal the land and sequester carbon. Allan Savory's work would be one world-class example.[1] We'll cover this much more in chapter 25 where we talk about how vegans can benefit from caring for cattle, chickens, hogs, etc. while maintaining their noble dietary choices.

Michael Pollan's book *The Omnivore's Dilemma* makes a strong point about veganism: you can actually kill fewer animals as an omnivore.[2] Farming practices for, say, conventional carrots, kill billions of animals and ground-nesting birds with all of the giant machines and poisoning involved. Raising a whole cow only requires one animal to die. The equivalent number of carrot calories might cost the lives of 500 small critters. The dilemma is, if you wish to minimize harm to animals, do you focus on the total number of deaths or total pounds of death? If you buy from a grocery store or restaurant, it is hard to be a vegan.

I want to reiterate that I have no problem with people choosing to be vegan. I just wish for them to understand that cattle and other animals can have a

1 permies.com/t/4334 (Allan Savory)
2 permies.com/t/1453 (*The Omnivore's Dilemma*)

positive impact on the environment and that the carrots found in grocery stores are not as innocent as they seem.

VORP – Expanding Our Vocabulary to Value Garden Food over Diet Cola

It has been my experience, after visiting with thousands of people, that some people thrive on a vegan diet and some people get really sick on a vegan diet. So, while I'm glad it's working for some people, I don't think veganism is a slam dunk for everyone.

Further, the studies that support vegan diets tend to universally compare a good healthy vegan diet (cooked well, using organic foods) to a western diet (non-organic, lots of sugars and processed foods). The equivalent from the opposite direction would be a study comparing something that the Weston A. Price Foundation[3] would approve as "omnivore" to the vegan side being represented by diet cola and "cookies." I think if you compare any wholesome diet to a non-wholesome diet, you will get the results you expect. There have been so many skewed studies that I now ignore any vegan studies unless the omnivores are represented with something at least as wholesome.

I bring up the "cookies" and diet cola because as much as veganism has some good ideals, the idea that these "foods" can be a part of the vegan diet really degrades the brand for me. Actually, the same goes for the omnivore diet.

Rather than insisting that the full buffet of dietary choice is limited to just vegan or omnivore, I think we need to open it up to thousands of choices. And then shift the discussion to:

- what are all the healthy choices?
- out of all the healthy choices for all people everywhere, which choice is best for you?

To talk about possible healthy choices, we need a word that filters out "cookies" (emphasis on the quote marks), diet cola, and other such "foods" – foods that are highly processed. But rather than saying "eat less highly processed food," I have chosen to embrace the word "virgin" to describe foods that are not highly processed so that I can say "eat more virgin food" instead.

In order to further facilitate this conversation, I came up with two new terms that embrace all of the values of organic with an emphasis on virgin foods: one for omnivores and one for vegans. First, there is "Virgin and strictly Organic" (VO), and then there is "Virgin and strictly Organic and Vegan" (VOV), which is a subset of VO. Diet cola and "cookies" would not make the cut for either.

The idea behind "organic" is to replace known toxins with things that we think are more natural and, hopefully, less toxic. Organic means:

- no GMOs
- no petroleum-based fertilizers
- no conventional pesticides (which includes herbicides, insecticides, fungicides, etc.)
- can include OMRI-approved pesticides (OMRI is the US government agency for organic labeling)

3 permies.com/t/2776 (Weston A. Price)

42

Most commercial organic operations are riding the edge of what is barely able to be called organic. And many would not even make the cut for "organic," but they were somehow able to get the label anyway…but that's not what this book is about.

Organic is about reducing toxins. Permaculture is about adding back in nutrition. We are only *beginning* to understand what we need for nutrition. Every few years, scientists come up with something that we didn't really know about before – sometimes about something we need that isn't in food as much as it used to be. So we find ways to compensate. There must be dozens or hundreds of things we still don't know about. For all sorts of problems, we are perpetually medicating ourselves with vitamins, lotions, herbs, or chemical medicines, either over-the-counter or prescription. It seems like damn near everybody is taking something for some problem.

Our biological existence comes from having evolved to eat certain foods within a hunter/gatherer society. In those days, 100% of the food people ate either came from a polyculture (an assembly of diverse species grown together), or from an animal that ate from a polyculture. Agriculture, as it would be recognized by the average person, started about 10,000 years ago.

And I wonder…what if damn near all of the ickiness would go away if we just replaced row crops with polyculture?[4] The poly-er the better.

I wish to convey something far beyond VO – something that embraces VO, but also has a strong emphasis on building rich soil and polyculture using permaculture. So I came up with "Virgin, strictly Organic, Rich soil, and Polyculture/permaculture." VORP.[5] (This word sounds so silly that I wish to somehow work it into regular conversation.) Since I made up the term, I get to define what it means.

VORP means:

- low processing, low packaging
- foods are grown in aged soil with a high organic matter level (more on this in chapter 17)
- polyculture of at least a dozen species
- harvested with minimal soil disturbance
- harvested by hand (no harvesting by machine)
- human-to-acre ratio is very high: more like gardening than farming
- super-localized inputs
- minimal irrigation[6]
- seasonal foods
- minimized grafting[7]
- super-localized plant and animal varieties[8]
- no cardboard or newspaper in horticultural endeavors[9]
- no pesticides, even OMRI-approved pesticides

4 permies.com/t/1427 (polyculture & health)
5 permies.com/t/vorp
6 permies.com/t/7292 (irrigation)
7 permies.com/t/1354 (minimized grafting)
8 permies.com/t/31939 (localized varieties)
9 permies.com/t/2157 (no cardboard/newspaper)

- growing plants in a space that suits them – as opposed to adding fertilizers and using pesticides to force an artificial environment
- pampered animals (bye-bye, CAFO)

When it comes to "building a better world" or your health, or nearly any set of values, I think that VORP is superior to old-school veganism, or any other dietary choice ever proposed. I think this silly word gives us traction for solving serious problems surrounding food choices.

When a Vegan Diet Has a Lower Carbon Footprint. And When It Doesn't.

In 2014, the movie *Cowspiracy* came out saying that the number one thing you can do for the environment is to become a vegan.[10] The biggest claim made in the movie was that animal agriculture causes at least 51% of all greenhouse gas emissions worldwide. Danny Chivers, climate change researcher and vegan, had this to say:

> "There's only one problem with this eye-grabbing stat: it's a load of manure. Emissions from livestock agriculture – including the methane from animals' digestive systems, deforestation, land use change and energy use – make up around 15 per cent of global emissions, not 51 per cent. I've been vegan for 14 years and have been asked to justify my dietary weirdness at more friend and family meals than I can count, so believe me – I've looked into it. If meat and dairy really were the biggest cause of global climate change I'd be trumpeting that statistic myself every chance I got."

Still, 15% is a big deal. It could mean that by switching from the Standard American Diet (SAD) to a vegan diet, a person could reduce their carbon footprint by roughly 4.5 tons! But that 15% comes from focusing on conventional ag (since that is how most meat is currently raised) and does not fully consider the possibilities of other techniques. To summarize a massive discussion,[11] here are some rough estimates:

Diet	Carbon Footprint (in tons)
SAD – purchased	10.5
Vegan – purchased	6
SAD with pastured animals – purchased	4.5
VORP omnivore – purchased	2
Vegan garden	0.5
VORP omnivore forest garden	-1

Rather than saying that everyone needs to be vegan for the sake of the environment, I think that, by advocating for VORP food, we can have a much larger impact. Then each person can decide whether or not to eat animal products, depending on what works best for them.

10 permies.com/t/101340 (*Cowspiracy* review)
11 permies.com/t/100593 (diet footprints)

GAT: Government-Mandated Acceptable Levels of Toxicity

I think that, in general, the best source for healthy, low-footprint food is going to be food that you are growing yourself and harvesting as fresh as possible. That said, not everyone has their own established permaculture/polyculture system. While I would like to encourage folks to garden (and we'll show you how to do it cheap and easy in chapter 17), I also know that there are folks who simply won't garden or won't produce all of their own food even if they try…and they still need to eat. And they'll probably still get their food from the grocery store. So how can people know what food at the store is going to be the best? At the store, the labels only say if food is organic or not.

This is the one and only point in the whole book where we will offer a political solution…so if that makes you really uncomfortable, you can just skip right on over to the next chapter and we'll be done with the political stuff. Pinky promise.

I was once interviewed for a radio show and told that I get to have one new law – so what is the one new law? My answer was that my new law would implement a more detailed food labeling system.[12] I would start by inverting the labels suggesting "normal" and "organic" – organic food would be labeled as "normal" and the food no longer called "normal" would be labeled as "Gub'mint decided it has Acceptable levels of Toxicity (GAT)." And rather than a black-and-white system like we have now (boolean: organic or not), this new system would be a real number system.

GAT food would be expressed numerically from 1.0 to 9.9. 1.0 would be "barely allowed to be sold as food for human consumption" and 9.9 would be "a tiny bit of toxicity." The new normal (formerly known as "organic") would be expressed numerically as 10.0 to 19.9. We could have values like 9.2 for something transitioning to normal and 16.9 for excellent VO products. VORP would start at 20.0, and maybe, eventually, we might have numbers as high as 50.0. Oh, and for anything below 10.0, the label would have to explain why.

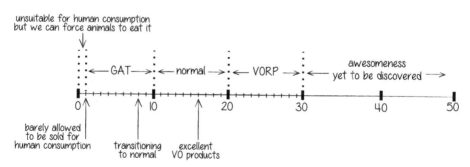

I think that with such a system, consumers would be able to make much more educated choices and, in addition, it would provide a solid incentive for producers to grow their food in a way that is healthier. Still, the best way to know the true story of your food is by growing it yourself.

Bonus political point: If you took away the chem-ag subsidy and the organic-ag penalty, the average consumer would pay four times more for chem-ag food.[13]

Back to our regularly scheduled nonpolitical programming…

12 permies.com/t/3093 (food labeling)
13 permies.com/t/16161 (food subsidies)

Part 3
Within the Walls of
Your Home

Chapter 13
REALLY Reducing
Home Energy Usage

This is the most critical part of the whole book. Reducing home energy usage addresses all three footprints and is the most applicable to the most people. Nearly all war is rooted in energy. Most pollution is rooted in energy. Energy has a huge impact on carbon footprint. Nearly all of our natural gas and coal footprints are from energy use. This chapter wrestles to the ground the biggest misconceptions in saving home energy. This chapter is THE game changer.

Unfortunately, there is an incredible amount of conflicting information out there as to how home energy usage actually breaks down.[1] Everyone seems to have their own set of numbers and a lot of it appears to be arranged in a way that is biased toward a particular point. An excellent example of this is when lighting is put into the "lighting & appliances" category where appliances happen to include such energy hogs as a clothes dryer, an oven, and a refrigerator. Conveniently, when a person sees that "lighting & appliances" is a rather sizable percentage, they often feel empowered to go out and buy some "better" light bulbs to drop that category down, totally ignoring the whole thing about energy hog appliances. Many of the charts also only include electricity usage, not energy usage, which is really convenient for helping those on natural gas feel better about themselves.

Based on summarizing dozens of conflicting reports about energy usage, here is a rough estimate for the breakdown of home energy usage in a cold climate:

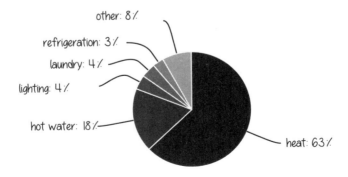

other: 8%
refrigeration: 3%
laundry: 4%
lighting: 4%
hot water: 18%
heat: 63%

1 permies.com/p/102770 (energy breakdown)

And for the average American:

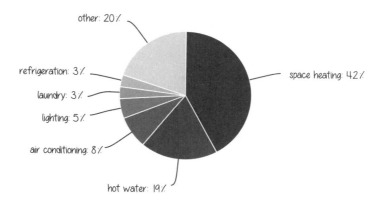

other: 20%
refrigeration: 3%
laundry: 3%
lighting: 5%
air conditioning: 8%
hot water: 19%
space heating: 42%

63% of Home Energy Use in a Cold Climate Is Heat

Looking at the numbers it is clear that we have, by far, the most to gain by reducing our heating costs.

How I Cut 87% off My Electric Heat Bill and Stayed Toasty Warm

In June of 2010, I moved to a place in Montana that had only electric heat. While living there by myself, I conducted experiments in cutting the amount of energy I needed to stay warm, with a focus on heating myself instead of heating the whole house.[2] Through using these techniques, I proved that I could save $500 per year on my heating bill.[3]

For the record, I am not a cold-hardened person. Some people have suggested that I can tolerate the cold better than most. And there might be a little truth to that, but only a little. Without using these techniques, I get uncomfortable at 65 °F (18 °C). In other words, at 65 °F – my fingers get stiff and I cannot type. Plus I just feel so cold that I cannot concentrate. And that is with a sweater on.

My optimized system ended up with two parts: my desk and my bed. The key is that when I am inside, I spend 99% of my time at my desk or in bed. I have had people comment on how this does not solve anything for families, or for people who are watching TV, or for people who live a life that does not follow this pattern. I think that this position has a lot of truth to it, but is not absolutely true. The key point here is that I focused on heating people instead of heating all of the air in the house. I think that this general approach can do great things for nearly every situation, although it could take some time and thought for each set of circumstances. Maybe some situations will be able to save only 50%. Others will be able to save 70%. Maybe somebody will have a situation where they are able to save 95%. Sweet.

2 permies.com/t/4906 (heat experiments)
3 permies.com/t/8388 (heat savings)

warm little pocket
when someone is sitting here

heat all of this air
to heat one person

At My Desk

Here is the general idea. Most folks heat the whole house to 72°F (22°C). My earliest efforts were to turn the house thermostat down to 50°F (10°C) and use a personal electric space heater to heat myself. That saved a lot, but it left my legs too hot and the rest of me too cold. Then I focused on "micro heaters" that would focus on warming me and not the whole room. I got this down to about 235 watts. And then I optimized the system where I added a sweater and focused the micro heaters on the areas featuring exposed skin or that seemed to get cold. I got this down to 82.5 watts.

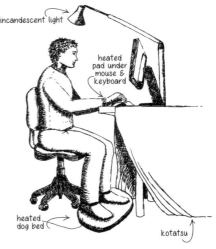

incandescent light

heated pad under mouse & keyboard

heated dog bed

kotatsu

I experimented with quite a few personal heating contraptions, and in time, optimized things down to these: a 15-watt dog bed heater for my feet, a 25-watt heated keyboard and a 2.5-watt heated mouse for my hands, and a standard 40-watt incandescent light bulb for my head. This last one was the most important. A standard incandescent light bulb heats something to the point that it glows white hot. So I used this to heat myself and it doubled as a light source. While I was optimizing my systems, somebody pointed out the value of the Japanese kotatsu (a popular low table with a built in quilted skirt and small heater under the table). So I added a blanket around my desk which helped hold some of the heat under my desk as I worked.

In My Bedroom

I had trouble getting to sleep in a cold room. And I really didn't like getting into a cold bed. I started to turn the heat up in my bedroom for a half hour before bed and then turn it back down as I got into bed. Once asleep, I was fine – I had lots of blankets. I later optimized this to using a heated mattress pad and a special timer. The mattress pad used 200 watts. The timer allowed power to pass through for 30 minutes and then it would shut off. If I turned it on, did something for 20 minutes, and then got into bed it was luxurious. After sharing this, I heard from dozens of people who have done similar things with hot water bottles – neat!

But What About … ?

There are so many different scenarios that providing the answer to each one would not fit in this book. If you are creative, you can likely come up with something that will work fairly well for almost any scenario.[4] Here are a few examples:

If you want to sit on the couch and watch some TV, one solution is to use a dog bed heater for your feet, a nice comfy blanket for most of your body, and a floor lamp with a swinging arm outfitted with an incandescent light bulb pointed at your head (probably directly above your head so you get all the warmth and the light isn't annoying anybody). That could be all you need to keep you toasty.

If you have kids who won't sit still…first of all, they will be warmer just because they are running around. If they're looking at a more low-key playtime, setting up a couple of dog bed heaters on the floor will go a long way to keeping them warm. In addition, some clever placement of incandescent light bulbs could light their play area and provide some extra heat to boot.

Turning the Central Heating down at Night (Fancy Thermostats)

I think this does produce some savings, but not as much as you might expect. If you set your thermostat to a constant 72°F (22°C), the heater works a little at a time throughout the day. If you drop it to 50°F (10°C) at night or in the middle of the day, the heater stops working, but then when the time comes to warm the house again, the heater has to work at full power for a long time to get the temp back up – thus losing a lot of your savings. A lot of people believe these fancy thermostats will cut 40% off their heating bill, and they are disappointed that it only cuts about 4% off.[5] I think people will get five to twenty times better results with keeping the temp lower all day and using micro heaters as needed.

The New Wood Heat: Smokeless and One Tenth the Wood

A Rocket Mass Heater (RMH) could be the cleanest and most sustainable way to heat a conventional home.[6] Some people have reported that they heat their home with nothing more than the dead branches that fall off the trees in their yard. And they burn so clean that a lot of sneaky people are using them illegally, in cities, without detection.

When somebody first told me about rocket mass heaters, none of it made sense. The fire burns sideways?[7] No smoke? If a conventional wood stove is 75% efficient, doesn't that mean the most wood you could possibly save is something like 25%? How do you have a big hole right over the fire and not have the house fill with smoke? I was skeptical.[8]

4   permies.com/t/108806 (micro heater scenarios)
5   permies.com/t/108807 (fancy thermostats)
6   richsoil.com/rocket
7   permies.com/t/70719 (sideways burn)
8   permies.com/t/72557 (RMH myths)

And then I saw one in action. The fire really does burn sideways. The exhaust is near room temperature – and very clean. The smoke doesn't come back up because a huge amount of air is getting sucked into the wood hole. Neat! I sat on one that had not had a fire in it for 24 hours – it was still hot!

How Does a Rocket Mass Heater Function Differently from a Regular Wood Stove?

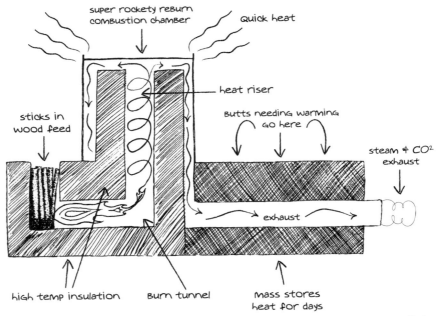

A regular wood stove will extract heat immediately. A rocket mass heater will direct the fire through an insulated space to make the fire burn much hotter before harvesting the heat. This burns the smoke and creosote in a controlled manner. Then most of the heat is extracted and put into the room. Any remaining heat is stored in a mass to be slowly released over the next couple of days.

The smoke coming from the chimney of a regular wood stove is typically 300 to 600°F (~150-320°C) and a large volume – typically stinking up the neighborhood. The exhaust from a rocket mass heater is typically 70 to 120°F (~20-50°C) and a small volume – usually clear and without odor.

How Can You Claim Such Crazy Efficiency? Wood Stoves Are Already 75% Efficient!

The question I am most often asked about RMHs is: "If my current wood stove is 75% efficient, it seems the most room for improvement is only about 25%. But you say you can heat a home with a tenth of the wood. Isn't that claiming that a rocket mass heater is 750% efficient? Wouldn't 100% efficient be the maximum?"[9]

First off, a rating of "75% efficient" does not account for some of the heat that goes up the chimney to remove the smoke. The testing labs will typically use a number of

9 permies.com/t/6199 (RMH efficiency)

16% for smoke going up the chimney. So the 75% number is actually 59%. Saying 75% is allowed in the regulations and sells more wood stoves.

Second, the rating of 75% was the most efficient result experienced in a laboratory with experts trying to get the most efficient numbers. While a wood stove might be able to achieve 75% efficiency in a lab, it rarely does in a home. An experienced wood stove operator will probably experience something more like 35%. Somebody using wet/green wood and shutting the dampers down a lot for a "slow burn" will probably experience something more like 5% efficiency (or less!) with a "75% efficient" wood stove, thus leaving a lot of room for improvement. Rocket mass heaters, by design, have no way to reduce the airflow for a slow, inefficient burn. An inexperienced wood burner will probably have a 90% to 95% efficient burn every time with a RMH.

Third, people who have replaced conventional wood stoves with a rocket mass heater have reported that they now heat their homes with one tenth the wood.[10] I heated my Montana home all winter with just half a cord of wood. This isn't lab evidence. This is real-life evidence.

How Does a Rocket Mass Heater Compare to Natural Gas or Electric Heat?

In general, for heating a home over a year, the CO_2 output for a rocket mass heater is 99% less than that of natural gas, which is 60% less than that of electric heat.[11]

The carbon footprint reduction of switching from electric heat to a rocket mass heater is the equivalent of taking 7 cars off the road every year! Also, even if you can't find some twigs and have to buy firewood, it still costs less to operate than natural gas.

Natural gas has a carbon footprint that is embedded deep in the ground. To use it, we need to un-embed it, and burning it puts carbon into the atmosphere. The same can be said for electricity generated by natural gas, coal, diesel, or propane – only more so.

A rocket mass heater uses wood – a renewable resource. If we don't burn it, that wood is going to decompose into the exact same carbon footprint. Further, in my area, if you don't burn the wood in a rocket mass heater, it will be burned in a very dirty way as either a wildfire or as a form of wildfire prevention.

What about the trees? The amount of wood used to heat a home with a rocket mass heater is so tiny that I doubt people will even bother to go out into the forest to get wood. Landscaping waste from an urban lot can be more than enough to heat a home.

Are These Things Safe?

A well-built rocket mass heater is safer than a natural gas heater, a gas stove, a gas oven, a gas water heater or anything in your home that is connected to natural gas. Also, if your wood pile has a "leak" you are much safer than if your natural gas system has a leak.

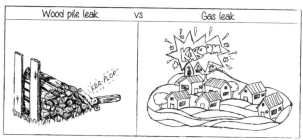

10 permies.com/t/59974 (half a cord)
11 permies.com/t/43271 (heat footprint)

Passive Heat Systems

Passive solar has ruled this space for decades.[12] And now we have some new offerings (coming in chapter 30) that can be used instead of, or with passive solar: passive annual heat storage,[13] wofati,[14] and annualized geo-solar.[15] These ideas can completely eliminate the need to heat your home with fuel. Instead, you are heating your home with sunlight, or you are capturing heat from the summer and using it in the winter.

19% of Home Energy Use is Hot Water

Boom Squish

After reading all the exciting stuff about the amazing qualities of a rocket mass heater, your mind may wander over to the question "Can I heat my water with that?" I wish to start by responding with yes…but don't try this without proper training first.

Building your own rocket mass heater is easy and safe. There are many excellent resources to guide you to happiness.[16] Rocket hot water is a very different story. If you try to do this on your own, and you do it with a pressurized system, there is about an 80% chance that you will die – and you might take others with you. Experts in this area tend to put a lot of effort in nonpressurized systems. This is one of those fields where you need a week of safety training before you start to build your first rocket hot water heater.[17]

An excellent episode of MythBusters bypasses the safety stuff on a standard hot water heater and the explosion is epic. I think their words were "That is the biggest explosion we have ever had on this show."

Boom. Squish. If there is no boom, then you won't be the squish. And then you will be able to buy more of my books in the future.

Making Your Hot Water Tank More Efficient

You might think that turning down the temperature on your water heater will save you money. Maybe you can buy an extra pizza each month! Nope! The sad news is, it won't even get you a lame cup of coffee. At the lowest setting of 110 degrees F (46°C), you might save $10 per year.[18] And you never get to take a hot bath. But it will also expose you to legionella bacteria, which are a significant cause of pneumonia.[19] The optimal reproduction temperature of legionella is 95 to 115°F (35 to 46°C), around the temperature some people like to lower their water heater to. I suggest that instead of putting your household at risk of getting really sick, you keep your water tank set to 140°F (60°C). And the next time that

LEGIONELA PARTY
When: Tonight at 115°
Where: Water heater

12 permies.com/t/108809 (passive solar)
13 permies.com/t/3033 (passive annual heat storage)
14 permies.com/t/wofati
15 permies.com/t/11604 (annualized geo-solar)
16 permies.com/t/63837 (my RMH DVDs)
17 permies.com/t/34547 (rocket hot water)
18 permies.com/t/107797 (hot water savings)
19 permies.com/t/2607 (legionella)

you need to replace your water heater, consider getting a smaller one. Also note that a lot of solar hot water designs are legionella bacteria incubators. Be safe!

Saving Hot Water Without Suffering Another Cold Shower

While we can make our water heaters more efficient, I believe the greater savings come from focusing on conservation. The more hot water you use, the more energy is consumed.

Common domestic hot water usage:

- Shower/bathing (40%)
- Laundry (30%)
- Dishes (15%)
- Washing hands (5%)
- Food prep (5%)

Using the mighty power of the English language, and nothing up my sleeves, I hope to reduce your hot water consumption by more than 65% while making your life more luxuriant! Lesser people are sure that it cannot be done, but read on and be amazed!

Nearly every attempt to convince people to reduce hot water usage suggests low-flow showerheads, colder showers, and "just be faster in the shower!" None of those suggestions make for a more luxuriant life. In chapter 15, we will talk about going 'pooless' in the shower: no soap or shampoo and yet not smelly.[20] More on the particulars of going pooless later, but the lack of soap or shampoo in the shower cuts my shower time pretty drastically – I just run out of things to do in there and get bored. The average shower length is 8.2 minutes. I'm at 1.2 minutes. That saves 85%!

Eliminating 100% of your hot water usage for laundry is easy. Most of the funk we are trying to get out of our clothes is water soluble – and cold water does the trick just as well as warm or hot water. Try it and see for yourself. If your clothes are covered in something oily, then, yes, warm or hot water will help. But that isn't the case for most people.

When it comes to washing dishes, the most important thing is what is the most luxuriant for you. But if we are going to take a moment to contemplate energy and water usage, let's unravel the marketing material designed to sell dishwashers. Even compared to the very best dishwasher in the world, I have a technique for washing dishes by hand that uses far less water.[21] But today we are talking about hot water because of the energy used. The dishwashers that use less water do so by using more electricity. An average dishwasher uses 1.5 kWh for one load – that is the same as 25 incandescent light bulbs (60 W) burning for an hour!

Do not fall for the "need" to sterilize dishes. That is fear-based marketing. You need your dishes to be clean – which is quite different from sterile. I believe that sterilizing your dishes actually reduces the effectiveness of your immune system.

Personally, I use my dishwasher as a drying rack for dishes I washed by hand. Sometimes I will feed a lot of people and then I will use the dishwasher to wash those dishes and be "a self cleaning drying rack." For me, the luxury is knowing that all of my dishes are clean. I don't have a dishwasher half loaded with dirty dishes and foody-bits

20 permies.com/t/pooless
21 permies.com/t/56138 (dishes)

that are slowly petrifying – and a stink wafting from this under-the-counter chamber of horrors. Others might choose to run their dishwasher two to five times more often to dodge this issue – but then they are REALLY wasting energy.

5% of Home Energy Use is Lighting

The average American household spends $80 per year on lighting. A few years ago I lived by myself and carefully measured every spec of electricity I used. My lighting use was $8 per year and that was all incandescent light. It's not terribly complicated, and I actually feel more comfortable when I use these habits.[22]

My neighbor had a large garage where a large boat was parked. My guess is that the boat was afraid of the dark – so a very bright light kept the boat company day and night. By far the biggest way to save on lighting costs, way more important than which light bulb you use, is to turn the lights off when nobody is in the room. Simple as that.

Next, move the lights closer to where you need them. For example, swinging-arm lamps for the desk and reading lamps for reading are best. Use reflective incandescent bulbs to direct light to a particular place rather than illuminating the whole room so much.

One 60 watt bulb gives off more light than four 15 watt bulbs. A long time ago, I had to split my power bill with my neighbor who had a medium-sized deck decorated with "lamp posts." Each "lamp" had 3 chandelier-style light bulbs. Six posts. Each bulb used 40 watts. 720 watts. A very pretty form of lighting that was left on 24/7. And when the 350 watt floodlight was turned on, it was far too bright and ruined the ambiance. Just to be clear: the 720 watts of little bulbs did not put out as much light as the single 350 watt floodlight.

You might think that installing dimmer switches on all of your light bulbs would be a great way to save power. While it does save some power, it turns out that there is not a linear relationship between the amount of current and the amount of light. If you dim a 60 watt bulb down to look like a 40 watt bulb, you are still using more power than it would take to power a 40 watt bulb.[23]

Lastly, work at ways to make better use of the free light coming from the sun.[24]

Good habits and a little knowledge about light and energy can cut your lighting bill 90%.

3% of Home Energy Use is Laundry

You stink. And washing your stinky self and your stinky duds makes it so the greater public never knows about all that stink. Congratulations, you sly dog!

I wish to give you two quick tips to help you in your romantic and professional quests to fool people into thinking you don't stink:

1. read the pooless stuff coming in chapter 15

2. for some reason, synthetic fabrics dramatically amplify your stink – so I encourage you to select a more natural wardrobe of cottons, silks, and wools.[25]

22 permies.com/t/31744 (lighting habits)
23 permies.com/t/85640 (dimmer switches)
24 permies.com/t/108811 (natural light)
25 permies.com/t/108813 (fabric and BO)

Shut the door! You're lettin' all the heat out!

If these two tips lead to you doing less laundry overall, then we're making progress! Of course, the luxurious life of not stinking comes way ahead of saving energy.

In the previous section, we already cut your hot water usage, but now let's move on to the biggest energy pig involving laundry: the clothes dryer. Earlier in this chapter, we made it clear that heat is the biggest energy pig in the home. A clothes dryer heats your clothes and then blows all that heat outside.

If saving over a hundred dollars in electricity isn't enough: using a clothesline or clothes-drying rack will make your clothes last ten times longer.[26] All that tumbling in your dryer wears your clothes out.

You might be thinking about what a hassle it is to take your clothes outside and put them on a line. And what if it rains? That's why I use a clothes-drying rack indoors.

Did you know that the word "pulley" was invented with a clothes-drying rack that would lift clothes up to the ceiling where it was warmer?

Some of you might be in an area that is quite humid. Good news! You now have a great excuse to run a dehumidifier! A dehumidifier typically uses much less energy than a clothes dryer and will reduce the humidity of your whole house while simultaneously drying your clothes!

The last point I want to make is something that you probably already know due to marketing: a front-loading washing machine uses half the water of a top-loading washing machine.

I think people using plenty of hot water and using the clothes dryer probably end up at about $200 per year in laundry energy cost per adult. And those people would be shocked to the core to learn that most Americans spend closer to $30 per year on laundry energy costs (this excludes detergent and paying for water). I have calculated that my annual laundry energy cost is now about $5.[27] That includes the power consumed to run the washer and the power needed to get cold water to the washer. And I am a giant guy with giant clothes, eating giant food that dribbles all over my clothes just below my giant pie hole. And, most importantly, I have a parade of people who want a picture of themselves in my armpit – those people have told me that I don't stink!

Put your face here

26 permies.com/t/dryer
27 permies.com/p/108825 (laundry cost)

The Little Things

Here are a few little things for those who want to tweak their savings even further:[28]

- Refrigeration – converting a chest freezer to a fridge can save 70% of refrigeration energy…but most people who travel this path get sick of crawling in to the refrigerator to get the things out of the bottom.[29]

- A haybox cooker can save energy and keep your home much cooler in the summer.[30]

- A rocket oven can help you convert a few twigs to something delicious like pizza, cake, lasagna, or pie.[31]

- A toaster oven gets small jobs done with far less energy than a full-size oven.

- Put a timer on bathroom fans.

- A plug-in kettle heats water with one-third the electricity of a stove-top kettle.[32]

- Put outdoor floodlights on a motion detector.

- A solar oven can do a lot of your cooking during the summer.[33]

The Physical Energy Footprint per Adult

In 2004, I worked for an aerospace company. We had 80 engineers and needed to hire 8 more, but we had no more space for cubicles. To start a new facility would be time consuming and freakishly expensive. I had an idea rooted in my philosophies of "more people in less space." I proposed an alternative.

There was a storage room with stuff in it. That stuff could be moved to a far cheaper, nonsecure location. The room could hold four small cubicles, but I proposed putting 16 people in there. I was told that that would result in the new people quitting, but I countered that it would hold the 8 new people, and not only would they not quit, but 8 of the existing engineers would request to move into this new workspace. And I would do the whole thing for less than $600 – less than the cost of the four cubicles. There was a lot of scoffing, and the sentiment was that my proposal was going to fail, so we were just wasting precious time in getting a new facility. I was allowed five days.

I recruited the help of a decorator, and we went to a few secondhand stores for inspiration. In the end, this space had three long tables and two small tables with workstations. Plus three couches, a few whiteboards, incandescent lamps, a wall of nerf guns, a pond, a fridge, posters of our spacecraft…the whole room was just packed with cool stuff.

I was right. People far preferred to work in there. We brought in *ten* more engineers, and several boring cubicles became empty.

Now let me bring this idea to the home front: Suppose you are moving into a home and you have your choice between two opportunities. They cost the same. One would mean that your bedroom would be massive – 14 feet by 25 feet (350 square feet).

28 permies.com/t/85742 (little things)
29 permies.com/t/31282 (chest fridge)
30 permies.com/t/8127 (haybox cooker)
31 permies.com/t/90191 (rocket oven)
32 permies.com/t/2429 (kettle)
33 permies.com/t/90518 (solar oven)

Just a standard room. White walls with beige carpet. And the other option is tiny – 10 feet by 10 feet (100 square feet), but it looks like it has been occupied by a wood carver for the last 100 years. It is a giant piece of art. Maybe it started as the captain's quarters in some ship from long ago. The bed is the centerpiece, on top of and nestled between dozens of drawers and art. It is explained to you that there are six secret compartments in all of this – good luck finding them!

What is *your* choice?

Some people will prefer the cubicle, or the plain white walls. And some will prefer the smaller footprint with some flavor of beauty/soul/art/culture.

One-third the physical footprint and a more luxuriant life. One-third the physical footprint typically means one-third the heat, one-third the light, and one-third the cleaning...plus a human body puts out 100 watts of heat around the clock, so if you pack more human bodies into a smaller space, your heating needs are reduced again. Not everything is cut by three, but a lot of things are.

As long as we are playing the mental exercise game, think about how the home size per person has nearly tripled since 1950.[34] That means in 1950, half of those people had an even smaller footprint. And I think that the footprint of today doesn't include the lonely boat figures (outbuildings).

 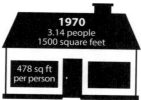 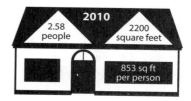

Along those lines, people all over the world are exploring the idea of living in a tiny house.[35] This is not for everybody, but some people have managed to reduce their physical home footprint by more than 90%. They eliminated their mortgage, and now a couple of light bulbs is all the heat they need.

And a few people are trying out the greatest possible experiment of all – sharing a space with other human beings...

34 permies.com/t/1765 (house size)
35 permies.com/t/1856 (tiny house)

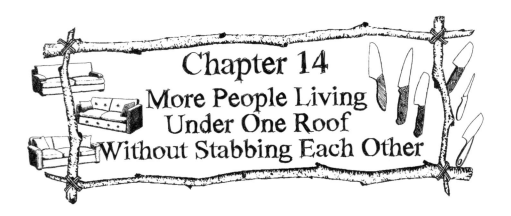

Chapter 14
More People Living Under One Roof Without Stabbing Each Other

This subject matter is 100 times more complex than everything else in this book combined, but it also has the potential to make the largest, most positive impact. The benefits of living in community are many. Oftentimes, the downsides to living in community are also many. We need to find a way to turn the volume knob up on the benefits and down on the drama.

Let's start by looking at the benefits and imagine a community where the drama knob is turned way down.[1] We have already talked in this book about how living in community can effectively reduce your footprint by as much as 60%. And we've also talked about how your living expenses might be cut in half. These benefits are huge! And there's more.

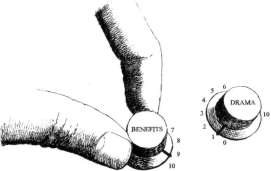

Imagine what it would be like to share three meals a day with the people you think are some of the coolest people in the whole world. I figure you'd become a ten-times-better person (by your own standards) just because of the awesome people you'd spend all of your time with. It would be like allowing yourself to drift down the river after a lifetime of paddling upstream. Those people you don't like – they'd be over in some other community with the people *they* think are some of the coolest people in the whole world.

When I lived by myself, 80% of my diet came from food that could be prepared in under a minute and was primarily a single course. I'm not a good cook. But I like a home-cooked meal made by somebody who knows how to cook. And maybe if I live in a house with twenty other people, some of them will be bonkers about cooking and make really amazing meals for the community sometimes. If cooking were divided evenly between all community members (which it doesn't have to be), each person would only have to cook once a week. And since they only have to cook once a week, they might put in an extra effort to make that meal extra special. So each person would cook twenty times less often and the food would be twice as good.

1 permies.com/t/community

Some people may be bonkers about gardening and choose to spend most of their time growing food for the community. Rather than spending money on groceries, the community could instead pay the gardeners in their community, either directly or through reduced rent. Others will love the career they are already in and might dabble in the garden but spend most of their time pursuing their career. That's the beauty of community. In many ways it can allow you to live an excellent life (fresh food, delicious meals, great company, drastically lower expenses, etc.) while you spend most of your time pursuing what interests you the most.

Another aspect that intrigues me about community living is that because of the much lower cost per person, extra money can be set aside to make the space beautiful. Nicer furniture, nicer appliances, nicer decorations, nicer everything. It would be like living in a piece of art.

I like sharing meals with lots of people. I like to watch movies with others. I like to sometimes play cards/games with others. I like to hear jokes. I like to learn about stuff. I like to share.

And then there is the challenging part: How do I turn the drama knob from a 9.7 down to a 0.5?

The answers won't fit in this book. In an effort of extreme brevity, here is a short summary of the top three things in my arrogant and obnoxious opinion:

"Obey or Else"

Most people NEED to hear their own opinion from all other people and are frustrated that they don't have the might to make it "right."

This can be summarized in three words: "obey or else."

It is easy to destroy community. It is almost as easy to build community.[2]

In order to build community, everybody must recognize that all human beings are hardwired with "obey or else" and that this frame of mind is poison to community. The only way to have community is for every member to recognize this and choose to build community, every day, despite this. Just being aware that this is THE poison for community could go a long way toward mitigating the problem. We have to consciously try to keep things together. Let's not have one person who is having a bad day destroy the entire community.

The Knives are in the Kitchen

My impression is that 90% of the problems in a household with several unrelated adults are rooted in the kitchen. If you come up with a food system that is dependent on people in the house being decent, you will learn the ugly truth: people are human.

I think that when coming up with a food system for community meals, you

2 permies.com/t/103249 (building community)

need a system where the foundation is that people are human. People will, by nature, seek the easiest path to put food in their belly.[3] Hunger is a powerful, driving force, and a full belly makes a human rather lazy. It is simply nature. It takes a rare, noble being to be better than this. And even the rare, noble being will not be perfect.

I think that if people are in the regular habit of being good and decent, and they are surrounded by people who are good and decent, they will become even more good and decent. Even generous. Exceptionally noble. But if people start down the path of disrespecting even one person in the community, the whole community may unravel into ugly chaos. And the odds are stacked 200 to 1 for the latter scenario.

There are many different ways to reduce drama in the kitchen. At one house I lived in, we had eleven people living under one roof. There was one woman there who was "queen of the kitchen." Basically, the policy was "it's her kitchen" and the rest of us were allowed to use the kitchen as long as we didn't upset her. And, since this was the expectation, there was much less drama.

Every once in a while, this woman pointed at somebody and said "you're not doing your share of the dishes, so you're going to wash everybody's dishes for two days." In other communities this could cause a major debate…but in our community it was her kitchen. If she said you weren't doing your share, then you weren't doing your share. It wasn't up for debate. Plus, everyone respected this woman because she was so generous to everyone – so generous that contesting her just didn't seem like a good idea because finding a better living situation elsewhere was not likely.

Dirty Cup CSI

When I first moved onto my land, we had what I call "the twenty-month party." In those twenty months, I had hundreds of people stopping by for a stay at my place. Some stayed for a few days and some stayed for a few months. The idea was to move my permaculture projects forward ten times faster than I could have by myself.

Some really neat stuff got done during those twenty months…and there was also a lot of drama. This drama had many facets, but one of the most draining was this: some people will be tidy, and some people will be pigs. Resentments will build and, eventually, resentments will tear the community apart.

We had a simple rule. When you finished drinking out of a cup, you were supposed to wash it immediately and put it away. That way there wouldn't be 20+ dirty cups in every corner of the house and none clean in the cupboard. This seemed like a simple rule that should be easy enough to follow and didn't require a huge effort. Apparently not. I would find a dirty cup and then go around trying to figure out who left their cup out so that I could ask them to clean it up. Unfortunately, people often opted to deny that it was their cup…even though there were multiple eyewitnesses that said they saw this person drinking from that cup.

This was happening all the time. Eventually I started calling it "dirty cup CSI." By the time I would finally nail someone and get them to confess and clean up the cup, they were pissed. I was pissed. Resentment built. In time, I came to see that dirty cup CSI did not fix things. No matter how much I tried to get messy people to be tidy, cups were still being left out.

There are a number of ways to solve this problem.[4] I'd guess that in most communities the solution will be this: charge slightly higher rent and hire a housekeeper who will come in once a week and clean up all of the common spaces. That way, the house will remain in an acceptable condition and a major source of drama will be removed. Then we can sit back and enjoy all of the amazing benefits that community has to offer.

4 permies.com/t/108819 (community home cleaning)

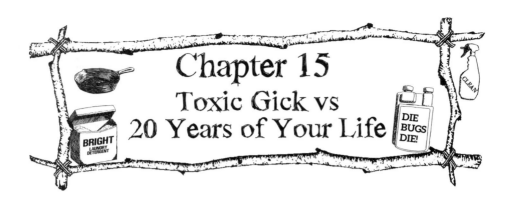

Chapter 15
Toxic Gick vs
20 Years of Your Life

A Better Cleaning Strategy Than Replacing Dirt with Poison

Stay-at-home parents are 50% more likely to develop cancer than parents who work outside the home.[1] The reason: toxic chemicals in household cleaning products. The exception to this is people who work outside the home as professional cleaners, who have it worse. Yikes!

Toxic cleaning products cause all sorts of health issues. Some people can hardly go out in public without getting a huge headache or breaking out in spontaneous hives because of some toxic chemical or another. For example, when I was younger, I used to get nose bleeds around laundry detergent, even just from walking down the laundry aisle at the grocery store. You might be dismissing these words now, but I promise that a lot of these issues are cumulative, and there is a high probability that your sensitivities will develop soon if they haven't already. Maybe you are suffering from something now, and you have not yet made the connection to the cause.

A few years ago, I watched the documentary film *Chemerical*.[2] It was about a family switching from toxic household cleaning and body products to more natural products. They hauled out four to six grocery bags of products from the house and then they tested the air quality in their home. Almost all of their rooms had way over the generally accepted safe limits of volatile organic compounds (VOCs). The mom was horrified.

At first, there was a lot of resistance to change. The mom was weeping. She kept asking how she would be able to clean things. At the end of the documentary, the whole family seemed dramatically healthier. And I don't really know how to express this, but they seemed…smarter. The mom went from being barely able to form sentences to being clearly articulate. By the time it was all over, she could not fathom ever using those old products again.

A really neat thing that they did in this documentary was to calculate the cost of the old toxic stuff: $239. The new stuff they bought, that wasn't nearly as toxic, was around $60 and just as effective. And the mom made a huge bucket of her own laundry detergent for just $2. Although I think there are better solutions than some of the ones

1 permies.com/t/108820 (cancer & cleaners)
2 permies.com/t/chemerical

mentioned in that documentary, the ones they presented are still far better than what was being used in the first place.

When considering what to use for cleaning, be wary of marketing fear tactics pushing sterility. There is a time and place for sterility, but it is not as much as what marketing people tell you. There are more bacteria cells in the human body than there are human cells. We cannot live without bacteria. So before you kill all bacteria willy-nilly, it would be wise to learn a little about good bacteria vs bad bacteria.[3]

Consider for a moment the bacteria that live in a septic tank and drain field or at the sewage treatment plant. If you pour something down the sink or into the toilet that kills them, they will not be able to do their very important job.

Here is a pretty complete list of cleaners I suggest:

- water, lots and lots of water – water alone is the best cleaner 90% of the time
- hot water
- boiling water
- vinegar
- baking soda
- citrus oils
- citric acid
- salt

- very small amounts of environmentally friendly soap
- very small amounts of environmentally friendly detergent
- hydrogen peroxide
- lots of fresh wash cloths
- a zip tool for clearing drains
- a pumice stone for scrubbing

As a final note: keep in mind that just because something occurs in nature, doesn't mean it is nontoxic or "good." Lead, arsenic, and cyanide are good examples.

Cast Iron Can Be Nonstick; Teflon Is Always Poison

I once heard about a person who was cooking with teflon (on a low temperature) and their pet birds died from inhaling the fumes – the birds' lungs filled with blood.[4]

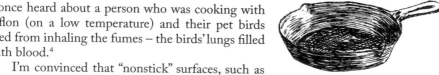

I'm convinced that "nonstick" surfaces, such as teflon, are toxic. Newer products come out that sound better, but I cannot help but think that folks just haven't yet learned how toxic the new surfaces are. At the time of this writing, I feel comfortable cooking with cast-iron, glass, and some steels.

Many of my happiest cooking memories involve cast iron.[5] I remember my grandad cooking almost everything we ate in a cast-iron skillet. My grandad was a really great guy, so I find I like to do a lot of stuff that he liked to do. For a long time

3 permies.com/t/118215 (good bacteria)
4 permies.com/p/22827 (bird casualties)
5 permies.com/t/154 (cast iron)

he was a professional mountain guide – how cool is that? And when he took me with him, the cast iron skillet would come with us too!

Using cast iron is a skill from a simpler time. It can last hundreds of years, while many modern skillets and griddles only last a few months. The best cast iron is the stuff that is already well used. Some people make a great score for $2 at a yard sale, and others end up dropping $80 on eBay. Even at $80, cast iron will earn its keep in less than a year.

Cooking with cast iron is one of those things where, at first, I failed utterly and repeatedly. It took seeking the wisdom of dozens of people, but I can now get that egg to slide off the skillet every time. A little knowledge and a little practice is all it takes.

Here are a few of my tips for cooking with cast iron:

1. Use a good cast iron skillet with a glassy-smooth cooking surface. The new cast iron with the rough cooking surface is going to be frustrating.

2. Keep it dry! Using water short-term (minutes, not hours) has its uses. When the time comes to put the cast iron cookware away, give it a few seconds on a hot stove, just to make sure all the water is out.

3. Use a little oil or grease.

4. A little smoke is okay.

5. Too much heat on an empty cast iron skillet can ruin the surface or even crack the skillet.

6. Clean cast iron immediately after each use and leave a very thin layer of oil/ grease.

7. Avoid soap! There is a myth about how you should never use soap on cast iron. The reality is that you can use soap on cast iron, but it is better if you don't.

8. Use a stainless steel spatula with a perfectly flat edge and rounded corners. This is what makes the cooking surface glassy.

9. The best way to season a cast iron skillet is just to use it. Going for a ride in the oven for the sake of "seasoning" is a waste of energy.

Going Pooless

For the uninitiated this might sound really weird, but for the last six years I have not used soap or shampoo in the shower…and I don't stink. I still shower every day, I just don't rub toxic gick all over my body as part of my shower routine anymore.

I am definitely not the only one who has tried this.[6] Millions of people with all sorts of hair length, color, and style have gone pooless and have never looked back. 98% of our funk is water soluble and thus can just be rinsed off.

Most people are concerned that, if they go pooless, their hair would be too greasy. Soap and shampoo strip away all of the natural oils being put out by our body. As a result, our bodies go into overdrive producing extra oil to compensate. And when we don't use shampoo for a day or two our hair gets really greasy because of the overcompensation. However, once we take the plunge and go pooless,

6 permies.com/t/pooless

our bodies adjust and stop producing so many oils. There is a bit of a transition period which varies from a few days to a few months depending on the person, but it all balances out in the end.

I recorded several podcasts about going pooless,[7] and a listener wrote to me to say that he tried it. After decades of daily migraines leading to vomiting and/or blackouts at least once a week, the migraines are now gone. After a month of being pooless, he used shampoo once and the migraines immediately returned. Is this man the canary in your coal mine?

With pooless we buy less stuff, so we have more money, and we are giving less money to the chemical factories…we use less water and use less energy for hot water… we have less toxic gick in our home, and we are putting less toxic gick on ourselves. Overall, we gain money and time, and we have improved the environment. We are building a better world in our backyard and making our lives more luxuriant along the way. Going pooless is one of my favorite examples of what this book is all about.

Bug Killer You Can Eat!

Depending on where you live, household pests can be a huge issue. Unfortunately, the conventional approach is to bring a bunch of poison into the house to kill the pests. And it usually doesn't even get them all. And the bugs and spiders that are the natural predators of those pests end up dying too.

Thankfully, there is a better solution that is so safe you can eat it! Despite all of the fancy poisons on the market, diatomaceous earth (DE) has been reported to be the most effective solution when fighting pests like fleas, ants, and bed bugs.[8] It is an off-white, talc-like powder that is the fossilized remains of marine phytoplankton. It kills nearly all bugs.

When DE gets on bugs that have an exoskeleton (such as fleas, ants, or bed bugs), it compromises their shell so that their innards turn into teeny-tiny bug jerky. At the same time, we can rub it all over our skin, rub it in our hair, or even eat it…and we are unharmed.

One strange thing to keep in mind about diatomaceous earth is that for it to work at killing bugs you have to keep it dry. Even morning dew can make it ineffective for this purpose.

I have encountered over a dozen ignorant people who have proclaimed "Diatomaceous earth does NOT work!" I have read this statement in all caps. In extra big fonts. With italics. And I've even had it screamed at me. On closer inspection of each case, there is always a flaw. Usually, the problem is that it was not used correctly. For example, DE is not a bait. If you put a little bit in a pile somewhere, the bugs are not drawn to it, and they do not invite all their friends.

The only known problem with food-grade diatomaceous earth for people, mammals, and birds that I have ever been able to find any reference to is breathing it in. I have heard from two people who said that they won't use DE anymore because "the tiny particles cut my lungs!" (deep sigh goes here) All I can say is "Did you actually examine your lung with a microscope and watch the diatomaceous earth cut into it?" Of course, they did not. I think the truth behind these reports is that these folks heard how diatomaceous earth works, and, when they breathed in the dust, it made them cough – just as breathing in flour or cornstarch would make you cough. And then they

7 permies.com/t/22356 (pooless podcast)
8 permies.com/t/2249 (Diatomaceous Earth)

thought of the sharpness at a microscopic level.

My understanding is that when diatomaceous earth becomes moist, the sharp thing is no longer happening. That's why you have to keep it dry when you use it as bug killer. As long as you are using **food-grade** diatomaceous earth you are quite safe, even if you breathe in gobs of it. Of course, if you are asthmatic, or have lung problems of any kind, I would think breathing in big gobs of any kind of dust would be a bad idea.

There exists another variety of diatomaceous earth that has been fiddled with so it can be used for pool filters. The pool-grade stuff would be bad for you because it contains up to 70% "crystalline silica." My understanding is that if you work with the pool-grade stuff all day, every day, for years, you could get cancer. **Don't mess with the pool-grade stuff!**

Food-grade diatomaceous earth will contain less than 1% crystalline silica and is far less dangerous. Many farmers feed it to animals and swear that the stuff kills all sorts of worms in their critters. And I've talked to a number of people keen on living past 100 who eat a quarter cup of food-grade DE every day. I have found references where it is cited for colon cleansing, parasite control, and detoxing. There are millions of people who are certain that eating this stuff makes for stronger fingernails, stronger bones, and more luxuriant hair. Further, nearly all grains are stored with some DE mixed in – to keep the insects under control without the toxicity. So not only is it far more effective at killing bugs than anything the pesticide companies have to offer, but you are already eating it – and millions of people choose to eat heaps more in the name of good health.

Part 4

More Than Half of Each Footprint Can Be Resolved in a Backyard

Chapter 16
The Huge Link Between Food and Global Footprints (Vegans Too!)

Growing your own food in a permaculture system can drastically reduce your global footprints.

No more petroleum-based fertilizers, no more petroleum-based pesticides, no more petroleum-powered machinery, and no more transporting food all the way to your table...using petroleum. Oh, and no more energy to produce, process, market, and transport fertilizers, pesticides, machinery, trucks, etc. either. On top of that, many ways that energy is used indirectly for food (building and powering grocery stores, food marketing, pesticide companies, law firms, fertilizer mines, and the millions of employees who work for all of these, etc.) are no longer contributing to your footprints. These savings could potentially reduce the average carbon footprint by a third[1] and cut the average petroleum footprint in half![2]

As a huge bonus, when we build soil instead of destroying it, we can effectively sequester carbon from the atmosphere into our soil. For example, in chapter 17 we'll talk about hugelkultur beds – essentially raised beds with rotting wood buried inside.[3] A lot of the carbon that was previously in the wood is incorporated into the soil instead of being released into the atmosphere.[4] The natural process of soil building is accelerated, we get delicious food, and we reduce our carbon footprint at the same time. Depending on how much of this kind of stuff you do and the amount of space you have, you may be able to reduce your footprint by 40%, 70%, 100%, or even reduce the footprints of other people!

Then there's the health factor. Conventional food is loaded with toxic gick. I think this plays a huge contributing role in all of our health problems. And when you go to the store, even if it's labeled organic, what is the true story of that food? Organic growers are still permitted to use pesticides, just ones that are considered "natural." And there are certainly enough stories out there that question the integrity of the organic labeling system...again, it's kind of hard to know what's really going on.

I prefer eating food that I've grown myself because I know the full story. I can know without a doubt that it was not sprayed with some kind of toxic gick and that it comes from a healthy, diverse polyculture. Plus, the nutrient quality of most food degrades as we wait for it to get from the source to our belly. By harvesting food in our

1 permies.com/t/90863 (food footprint)
2 permies.com/t/petroleum
3 permies.com/t/hugelkultur
4 permies.com/t/50725 (hugelkultur sequestration)

backyard, we can pack more nutrients into our body, and the food tastes better.

In addition to the possibility of lower medical bills, growing your own food can result in other significant savings as well. Can you imagine not paying for groceries? That's a lot of money we could use for something else! If done right, the costs of growing your own food can be miniscule when compared to the benefits. For example, if you spend $1 on a packet of seeds, you might get $10, $100, or even $1000 worth of food out of it! And if you save your own seed you can even eliminate those costs and grow varieties that are better adapted to your site.[5]

A lot of people want to compare the time it takes to buy food at the store versus growing a garden. And growing a garden seems like a huge time commitment. I think traditional gardening *is* a huge time commitment, which is why I prefer to follow the permaculture path. In the next chapter, we'll address this issue by talking about ways to grow double the food with one tenth of the effort.

If we're going to do a proper comparison, what we really need to consider is that when you buy food from the grocery store there is time involved too. First of all, you need to get there. Then you have to look for your food and put it in your cart, wait in line, tally up your purchases, and pack it home. Plus there's this: In order to buy groceries, you need money. And in order to get money, most people exchange their time for money at a job that they might not particularly enjoy. Rather than working at a job that I don't like, I think spending time in the garden is far more enjoyable.

Now, to be fair, you might not necessarily be able to grow all of your own food where you live. For example, if you have ¼ of an acre (~1000 m²) of an urban lot and you bring in no inputs from off-site (I have a whole host of concerns about importing materials), you will likely only be able to grow half your food.[6] And you're probably not going to be growing much animal protein in the city – so you'll have to buy that from somewhere else. Unless, of course, you are vegan. Then you will have to buy more grains and vegetables from somewhere else.

It's still important for people in the city to grow food – it makes a big difference. And the biggest difference will be with a bigger plot of soil – big gardens can produce more than you eat. If you feed yourself and sell or give away a million calories of food, then just through the act of gardening (and nothing else), you may have offset 100% of your petroleum footprint, 100% of your toxic footprint, and 70% of your carbon footprint. With a few more fruit trees, zucchini plants, salsa, and jams, you might be displacing the footprints of several people!

There are many ways to build a better world. The most effective is permaculture gardening.

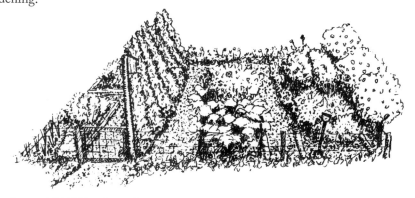

5 permies.com/t/31939 (seed saving)
6 permies.com/t/51153 (urban food)

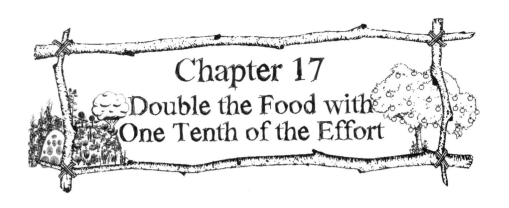

Chapter 17
Double the Food with One Tenth of the Effort

When I was a little boy, I was tasked with pulling weeds in the garden. There were so many other things I would rather be doing. When I entered adulthood, I was pretty well set against gardens. And then things happened, and I found myself obsessed with gardening. That obsession expanded into permaculture, and the fruit of that obsession is this book.

At the same time, I am freakishly lazy. As the decades passed, I found others of a similar mindset, and we would swap recipes for lazy gardening. It appears there are millions of lazy gardeners all over the world practicing these techniques. Compounding these techniques with authentic effort is now greening deserts[1] and feeding millions.

For the sake of this book, I wish to share just enough to give you a taste of what can be.

A great example of what I'm shooting for is a single apple tree in somebody's yard. You have probably seen the very apple tree I am talking about. The tree gets zero care and yet once a year there is a massive bounty of magnificent apples. Yet orchards require massive care: spraying, mowing, spraying, irrigation, spraying, pruning, spraying, grafting…but mostly spraying. Lots of money and time. As a lazy person who is cheap and also wants to avoid the stuff in the sprays, that neglected tree is looking pretty good. My twisted mind starts to think "how can I do something like that for nearly all of my food?"

The steps for growing a normal garden in a cold climate are:

- Start seedlings
- Prepare the soil in spring
- Plant
- Irrigate
- Fertilize
- Weed/insect/fungus control
- Harvest
- Clean up the beds in fall

1 permies.com/t/2584 (greening the desert)

The recipe for the apple tree was to make the harvest bigger, and eliminate all the other steps. Did the apple tree ever have any of the other steps? Years before we admired it? Did somebody prepare the soil and plant the tree? Maybe. I choose to believe that the tree grew from a seed from an apple core tossed on the ground.

Corn, however, cannot reproduce without human intervention. If people stopped planting corn, corn would be gone in two or three years. So not everything can be as easy as an apple tree.

Using the foundations of basic gardening and just a few pages, I will now attempt to reduce effort to one tenth and double the harvest. I feel a little bit like a magician standing on a stage announcing the trick. And my beautiful assistant is Shawn. Say hi, Shawn. ("Hi!") The secret behind this trick is not a single sleight of hand, but dozens of little things that all add up to one big performance!

Transplanting? That's Unnecessary Work!

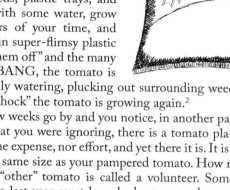

The icon of gardening is the tomato. Pizza, tacos, or burgers just wouldn't be the same without tomatoes. And I've heard rumors of people eating something called "salad" with tomatoes.

People will buy tomato seeds, plastic trays, and potting soil. Mix them all up with some water, grow lights, six weeks, and ten hours of your time, and PRESTO! Little tomato plants in super-flimsy plastic pots. Skipping over "hardening them off" and the many debatable ways to transplant – BANG, the tomato is now planted in your garden. Daily watering, plucking out surrounding weeds, and… after 7 to 14 days of "transplant shock" the tomato is growing again.[2]

A few weeks go by and you notice, in another part of your garden that you were ignoring, there is a tomato plant. It had none of the expense, nor effort, and yet there it is. It is currently about the same size as your pampered tomato. How rude.

This "other" tomato is called a volunteer. Some tomato plant from last year must have had a tomato drop unnoticed. The little seeds waited through the winter and then some seeds germinated earlier than others. Maybe there were fifty little baby tomato plants, but only one survived to this point. Most gardeners have observed that the volunteers typically outperform the coddled plants – they are bigger, stronger plants with more fruit. They get a later start, but they don't go through transplant shock. Further, a tomato has a taproot that can find resources very deep in the soil – but transplanting kills the taproot. Volunteers still have their taproot.

Permaculture is a more symbiotic relationship with nature so I can be even lazier. Which path is more aligned with nature? Which path is lazier? That volunteer tomato is singing my lazy permaculture song.

Most transplanting for any species can be replaced with direct seeding.[3] And when you have been gardening long enough, you start to get lots of volunteer squash, melons, lettuces, and fruit trees – food plants become your "weeds"!

2 permies.com/t/101018 (direct seeding vs transplanting)
3 permies.com/t/2394 (direct seeding)

Prepping the Soil to Not Need Prepping

Most people run a rototiller on their garden every spring. It destroys a lot of the "weeds" that are getting started, and it makes for a fluffy soil that is easy to plant in. And the garden plants LOVE it! Oh, sure, that tiller was crazy loud, extra stinky, and definitely a long way away from nature, but look at how much the growies thrive on freshly tilled soil…for the first year or two.

Every time you till the soil, you lose 30% of the organic matter (microbial soil life is killed and the plants feast on their dead bodies).[4] In other words, every time you till, you bring your garden closer and closer to being a cement-like dirt that nothing will grow in. You are sacrificing your future for the sake of this year's garden. This is why people with older gardens will till in manures – to replace the organic matter lost with previous tilling.

Eventually, people get tired of tilling and bringing in mountains of manure, so they switch to no-till, raised-bed gardens.[5] By not walking on the gardens, the gardens are less compacted and the growies can have all of the happiness from till, without all that effort. Aged soil loaded with organic matter soon becomes loaded with earthworms that provide far more benefit than the tiller ever did. And a raised bed that is two feet tall will typically add two weeks to both ends of the growing season because cold air tends to hug the ground. In time, raised beds need far less water and far fewer nutrients. A strong win for the lazy gardener!

After 15 years of improving my techniques with raised beds, I learned about hugelkultur: raised beds with wood buried inside.[6] As the wood rots, it provides a massive sponge for soil microorganisms, nutrients, and water. The sponge can be so massive that eventually you can eliminate the need for irrigation and fertilization! And that rotting action makes the wood shrink, leaving behind air pockets – a bit like the air pockets you would get from tilling. The ultimate raised-bed garden!

4 permies.com/t/564 (tilling losses)
5 permies.com/t/42 (raised beds)
6 permies.com/t/hugelkultur

Hugelkultur is a gift to your future self. Take the effort you would have put in with that rototiller and manure, mix in the hugelkultur recipe, and you have the rough shape. Next, mix in all the garden care you would have put in for that first year of the tilled garden and you have a giant step forward. Next year there will be one tenth the effort, and in the third year there will be one twentieth of the effort. In those years, you can use your extra energy to build more hugelkultur beds. Or just lie in a hammock and watch the clouds pass.

> ### Long-Term Carbon Sink
> "Biochar (charcoal) from wildfires can help soil hold more water, nutrients, and soil life for 1000 years! You can do this yourself.[7] No wildfires needed!"
> - Greg Martin, biochar.com

Planting Once and Harvesting for Years

It seems to me that most of the time when someone is growing some of their own food, their gardens are almost exclusively annual plants. This means that every year they plant up to 100% of their garden from scratch. If you're just growing a couple of tomato plants and a few carrots, that might not matter too much. On the other hand, if you're trying to grow a huge garden, planting can be a lot of work!

A key component of a permaculture garden is a much larger focus on perennial plants.[8] One reason is that perennial plants are typically more resilient than annuals once established – they've stored up energy from previous years that can help them get through a rough year.

Depending on where you live, there are any number of edible perennials that can be included in your garden, both woody plants like apples, plums, and hazelnuts and non-woody plants like asparagus, broccoli,[9] and sunchokes.[10] The idea is to plant once and reap the benefits for years to come.

While focusing on perennials really brings the work down, we can still have a fresh garden tomato once in a while. But rather than doing all of the work myself, I like to encourage my annual plants to seed themselves among the perennials. And rather than harvesting all of the seed and then planting it again next year, I just let it fall where it may. If it grows, great. If not, no harm done. Either way, very little to no planting is required on an annual basis.

Mulching 2.0: Being Naked Is No Longer Required!

Ruth Stout[11] is famous as "The Queen of Mulch," and equally famous for gardening naked. She pioneered a gardening technique that she called "no work gardening." Instead of tilling and composting and the other things that most gardeners do, she just put a whole lot of hay down and threw her seeds and compostables under the bits of hay. She did nothing else but harvest. As the years passed, she added seeds, compostables, and a bit more hay. Her garden became more glorious with each year.

Decades later, people use all sorts of different things for mulch: straw, rocks, wood

7 permies.com/f/190 (biochar)
8 permies.com/t/96847 (perennials vs annuals)
9 permies.com/t/21304 (perennial broccoli)
10 permies.com/t/sunchokes
11 permies.com/t/10360 (Ruth Stout)

chips, sawdust, twigs, leaves, bark, compost, coffee grounds, grass clippings, pine straw, and, of course, hay. And we have learned that some growies like certain mulches better than others: strawberries like straw (go figure) and raspberries are especially keen on wood chips.[12]

Hay is nearly perfect for most crops.[13] It is loaded with nutrients, so that each time it rains it's as if the growies get a perfect cup of fertilizer tea. The hay provides magnificent earthworm food and shelter. A few plants will find that hay has a bit too much fertilizer, but most plants find it to be exceptionally delicious. The only mulch that might be better is homemade compost.

After Ruth Stout died, nearly all hay, straw, and compost was made unusable for gardeners. But it's not Ruth's fault! Persistent herbicides gradually gained popularity. They have a half-life of 7 to 11 years and are found to be handy for people growing hay or grass crops. These persistent herbicides will kill any plant that is not a grass. I suspect that most of your garden is not grass. So when you put hay or straw on your garden today, there is a 96% chance that your garden will die. Nearly all commercial composts also have enough persistent herbicide residue to stunt or kill your garden.[14]

The moral of the story is that mulch is excellent for our quest. And the best mulches have now become mostly unavailable to us. You can find usable hay and straw – or grow your own. And you can even make your own compost. But this sorta shifts the work from old-school, labor-intensive gardening to a whole different type of work.

And as long as we are tempering the magic of mulch: Ruth had a LOT of rainfall in her area. I think that mulch combined with some extra rain and magnificent garden soil definitely does the trick. For those of us with less rain and beginner soil, ample mulch will need to be combined with some other tricks.

Many people in the permaculture world love advocating the use of newspaper or cardboard as a mulch material. And while I think it is possible to make newspaper or cardboard that would be safe (by my standards) for gardens, most use toxins that I am not comfortable with.[15] Some people have recipes for making these materials "safe" by peeling off the tape, or selecting only black and white pages, but my issue is with the chemicals used to make the paper or cardboard – so the toxicity is throughout the material, not something that can be scraped off. I have a lot more concerns about these materials, but the grand summary is: don't.

My favorite mulch today is "chop and drop."[16] Most of my garden has already been mulched and the only plants growing there are plants that I have encouraged. For the parts of the garden where I didn't have enough mulch yet, there are things growing there that I don't want. So I cut the things I don't want, and, rather than hauling it away or to a compost pile, I make a thick wad and place that wad on top of other stuff I don't want – effectively smothering it. It is far faster than driving far away to get a load of pristine hay, parting with money, and then hauling that hay to where I will use it in the garden. Chances are that what I am chopping is not a grass – thus proving that it is free of any persistent herbicides!

12 permies.com/t/3702 (raspberries)
13 permies.com/t/9191 (hay as fertilizer)
14 permies.com/t/57773 (toxic compost)
15 permies.com/t/2157 (toxic paper)
16 permies.com/t/46259 (chop and drop)

I also use rocks, sticks, twigs, pinecones, rotten logs, and sawdust as mulch.[17] Wherever there is something from nature I wish to get rid of, it can almost always work as a mulch if I can't find a better use for it somewhere else. And if I don't have chickens or pigs to take kitchen scraps, they go under a bit of chop-and-drop in the garden – just like what Ruth Stout did.

3D Gardening – Big Berms Bring Big Benefits

A few years ago, I was asked to speak to about 50 master gardeners in Great Falls, Montana. It was my first time to Great Falls. As you stand in Great Falls and look west, you can see the Rocky Mountains. And when I say "stand" I mean that you should be sure to lean into the wind.

In many ways, the climate of Great Falls is the same as Missoula. Temperatures are about the same, precipitation is about the same, and the elevation is pretty much the same. The only big difference is the wind. Missoula is in the middle of the Rocky Mountains, and Great Falls is part of the Great Plains with a view of the Rocky Mountains.

I visited a few farms and gardens. As you look far in every direction, there are hardly any trees. The only trees I could see were Russian olive – a tree famous for tolerating extremely dry conditions.[18] The area around Missoula is covered with trees.

Wind is desiccating (drying) and cooling. I recorded a podcast there while standing on a small suburban lot.[19] The backyard was a little bigger than an urban backyard. The woman who lived there told me she could hang wet clothes outside, and it would take about ten to fifteen minutes until they were dry.

My #1 bit of advice for her was to make tall berms: piles of dirt and soil about 15 feet (~5 meters) tall.[20] Just within her fence line. And, near the top of the berms, plant trees that can tolerate desert conditions. All of the neighborhood would be able to see her new jungle. Neighborhoods from ten miles away will probably be able to see it! And between the berms would flourish a magnificent jungle garden. At least it would appear to be jungle-esque compared to her neighbors. In time, I think she would not need to water it. A decade later, the properties next door would start to develop jungle-like attributes.

She will never eliminate the wind, but she will be able to eliminate 95% of it.

15 Feet

17 permies.com/t/105747 (kinds of mulch)
18 permies.com/t/33678 (Russian olive)
19 permies.com/t/17064 (Great Falls podcast)
20 permies.com/t/berms

So we have now created a spot that is moister and warmer, which means less irrigation and a longer growing season in Montana. But this is just the beginning.[21]

The south-facing slope of the berm will be, overall, warmer than the north-facing slope. So plants that love heat, or a long growing season, will have a home, and plants that prefer things to be cooler will also have a home. And plants that tolerate both will ripen at different times and have different flavors.

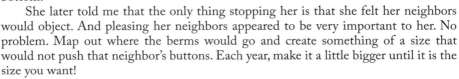

When the rain falls on flat land, everything

Berm Cross Section

gets the same amount of water. When rain falls on a berm, the water tends to be shed from the peak and accumulates at the bottom. Plants that do better with dry conditions will flourish at the top, and plants that need lots of water will be comfortable at the bottom.

She later told me that the only thing stopping her is that she felt her neighbors would object. And pleasing her neighbors appeared to be very important to her. No problem. Map out where the berms would go and create something of a size that would not push that neighbor's buttons. Each year, make it a little bigger until it is the size you want!

How Trees Nurture Gardens, Cool Your Home, Heat Your Home, and Save the World

Permaculture systems have a lot more trees than most gardens. Conventional gardens emulate conventional farms – they are flat and have few trees for the convenience of the machinery. Once we eliminate the machinery, we can "un-flatten" the land and add trees back in. This way, we can take advantage of the superpowers of trees in our garden.

For starters, trees are typically the most resilient and reliable food-producing plants. They keep producing year after year with very little care. Trees can usually handle much more adverse conditions than herbaceous plants. For example, once established, people with an apple tree in their yard are likely going to get apples every year until the tree dies – and the tree may live longer than you do. Trees also often provide the best nectar source for honey.

Trees accelerate the benefits of polyculture by sharing water and nutrients from deeper in the soil with surrounding plants. They also act as giant water pumps, pumping water from their roots all the way up their trunks into their leaves. Most of this water transpires out of their leaves and significantly raises the humidity in the area. Because of this, water that was once not available to shallow-rooted plants now becomes available because of the presence of a tree. And if you add in a couple of berms to reduce wind, even more of the moisture will stick around for all the plants.

When a forest is cut down, local creeks usually dry up shortly thereafter. That's because trees play such an important role in slowing and soaking water into the soil rather than allowing it to run off. By doing the reverse and planting enough trees in and around dry gullies, we can bring back streams![22] If that tidbit wasn't cool enough for you, here's another one: Trees create rain. An excellent example is Willie Smits' work, where he was able to increase the rainfall in an area of Borneo by 20% in only

21 permies.com/t/16894 (longer growing season)
22 permies.com/t/3416 (healing gullies)

three years – mostly just by growing trees as part of a polyculture![23]

Another excellent benefit of deciduous trees is that they produce enormous amounts of mulch that are delivered straight from the tree to your garden every fall – free of charge.[24] This helps feed the soil in all the wonderful ways mentioned earlier in this chapter.

Trees also reduce evaporation, partially because they act as a bit of a wind barrier (though not as good as berms),[25] and partially because the shade helps keep the sun off the soil. This works well because many plants have evolved to grow in the partial shade beneath a tree, and many food crops will produce more with a bit of shade than if they have a full day of sun.[26]

With proper use of tree shade, we can keep the sun out of our homes in the warmest months, possibly eliminating the need for an air conditioner.[27] In the colder months, the leaves fall off the trees and allow the sun in, warming the house.[28] Of course, there's a bigger way trees can heat your home – with a rocket mass heater.

But wait! There's more! Now free with every tree comes a massive solution to the carbon footprint game. There is a bit of uncanny math between trees and atmospheric CO_2: Trees convert about one ton of atmospheric CO_2 into one ton of tree matter. And one ton of tree matter will, eventually, transform into about one ton of atmospheric CO_2 (typically through fire or decomposition).[29] With a pocketful of tree seeds, you can offset your own carbon footprint in an afternoon. Repeat a dozen times and you have offset the carbon footprint of a dozen people.

A huge chunk of our carbon footprint comes from cutting down or burning rainforests to make room for conventional agriculture.[30] Yes, yes, I know that you, personally, did not cut down any rainforests. But we both know who bought that food. And now you know why I am so passionate about folks growing their own garden.

Long ago, far more land was covered in jungle and forests. If more carbon is locked up in a giant jungle (or forest), the result is less carbon in the atmosphere.

Here's an odd thing to consider at this point: If you build a log cabin, that postpones the decomposition of those logs by 80 years. You have sequestered more carbon. The same can be said for anything made of wood that will have a long use cycle.

Oh! That reminds me of another benefit of trees: wood!

Replacing Fertilizer with Polyculture

About 20 years ago, I bought 80 acres (~30 hectares) from a hay farmer. He was selling the property because the cost of fertilizer got to be more than he earned selling the hay. And that doesn't even take into account having to get the fertilizer to the farm and apply it.

I would like to have infinite free fertilizer. And I would like to not have to go get it and apply it. I will do a little bit of work up front with about twenty things so that I will get all the free and effortless fertilizer, but the tippy top thing in this list is "polyculture."[31]

23 permies.com/t/8596 (Willie Smits)
24 permies.com/t/97296 (fall leaves)
25 permies.com/t/108856 (windbreaks)
26 permies.com/t/76253 (plants for shade)
27 permies.com/t/14038 (house cooling)
28 permies.com/t/108809 (passive solar)
29 permies.com/t/108857 (CO_2 conversion)
30 permies.com/t/108859 (deforestation)
31 permies.com/t/64412 (polyculture)

In order to have the word "polyculture" we need to have the word "monoculture."[32] A monoculture is where you might have an acre of carrots. All one thing. A lame polyculture might be two different species mixed together. A magnificent polyculture would be fifty different species all mixed together.

As the centuries have passed, farmers have gained some idea of what to add to the soil to make for a good-looking, marketable carrot (which might be different from a healthy and nutritious carrot). The farmer would test the soil each year to make sure that the amendments were optimized. A lot of work.

Each carrot takes what it needs and wants from the surrounding soil. And, each carrot exudes stuff from its roots (carrot poop – technically called "exudates").[33] In a monocrop, the only stuff that is available to the carrot is what the farmer provided and the exudate of neighboring carrots.

I believe that the best carrots are fed the stuff that the farmer has figured out, PLUS a few hundred other things. Research has shown that, in a polyculture, the carrot will take in the exudates of other species. But what it does not want is the exudate of other carrots. So other plants generate carrot food and take away carrot poop.

Further still, research has shown that certain foreign substances, when given to one plant, can be detected in plants twenty feet (six meters) away several days later.[34] The substance was exuded and taken up by several plants to eventually reach the plants twenty feet away.

But it gets better! Mushrooms are the fruiting bodies of fungi. Most of the life of fungus is as webby stuff in the soil called mycelium. And fungus loooooooooves sugar. But without green leaves, mycelium has no way to make its own sugar. It depends entirely on the sugary exudates of plants. But the wacky thing is that mycelium *trades* stuff for sugar.[35] While the mycelium can trade some minerals it has managed to mine, its favorite item to trade is the exudates of other plants or microorganisms ("if you give me sugar, I will give you…mystery poop!"). Research has shown that the amount of exchange between plants increases tenfold when the soil is rich in mycelium. It can take months or years for mycelium to get to its full power – which is another great reason to not till.

As a bonus, this combination has a powerhouse of additional features including reducing the need for irrigation (tap-rooted plants get more water and share) and optimizing the amount of sunlight each plant gets (most plants prefer less than full sun and end up getting a little shade from bigger plants). There are a dozen more benefits, and probably a dozen more on top of that to be learned about as these techniques become more popular.

Monocrops Need Pest Control; Nature Doesn't

Most modern organic farming practices are very similar to modern chem-ag practices – only the fertilizers and pesticides are replaced with OMRI-certified products.

Suppose you have a 40-acre (~16-hectare) field of organic potatoes and you see Colorado Potato Beetles.[36] As a farmer, you better do something or you will lose your crop. It will not be possible to pick the beetles off by hand, so the OMRI-certified pesticides are starting to look very tempting.

32 permies.com/t/106312 (some definitions)
33 permies.com/t/102935 (exudates)
34 permies.com/t/108861 (nutrient transport)
35 permies.com/t/83769 (nature's internet)
36 permies.com/t/8652 (Colorado potato beetles)

An important note at this point is that the 40-acre field is flat – to be tractor friendly. All of the potatoes get the same amount of sun, water, and fertilizer. The pH, organic matter levels, and everything else about the soil is all about the same. And, of course, it's a monocrop.

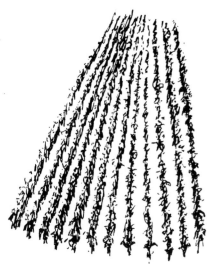

A permaculture system is a polyculture. The land is not just full of 7-foot-tall (~2 meters) hugelkultur beds, but a few 15-foot-tall (~5 meters) berms too.[37] And not only is it a polyculture, but there are trees mixed in. Including a few really big trees. All of those variations create a lot of diversity in how much sun each plant gets. Rainfall tends to run off the tops of things quickly and puddle in the low spots. What is inside the hugelkultur is quite wacky – different kinds of woods, soils, some kitchen scraps here, some hay there…maybe some big logs in that one, and just little twigs in this one. Different types of mulch and soil history make it so there is as much diversity on the inside as the outside.

On top of all this, remember: permaculture is a more symbiotic relationship with nature so I can be even lazier. If I see a Colorado Potato Beetle, that beetle is part of nature. That beetle has a job to do in the garden: to take out plants that are doing poorly.

Since my garden is not all the same, then it makes sense that there will be potatoes in a spot that is great for potatoes. And there will be potatoes in a spot that is not great for potatoes.

If I see Colorado Potato Beetles doing their job, they are helping me out. They are removing the potatoes that are in a spot that is more suited for, say, carrots. So the potatoes come out and the carrots thrive. Thanks, beetles!

In other parts of my garden, the potatoes are in a good spot for potatoes. So the potatoes thrive, and the beetles don't bother them.

The organic monocrop farmer will lose the entire crop if something isn't done. I, on the other hand, do nothing and still harvest heaps of potatoes.

Let's Do the Math

The title of this chapter is "Double the Food with One Tenth of the Effort." Is it truly possible? Well, how much time does it take to grow a garden the conventional way? How much time does it take to grow a garden the permaculture way? The answer to these questions is the same answer to "how long is a piece of string?" The answer is "it depends." Here is my attempt at a solid answer:

Bob and Alice are neighbors. They have both been gardening for five years. Bob has chosen the conventional path and Alice has chosen the permaculture path. Their yards receive the same amount of sunlight, the same weather, and, by some stroke of luck, they have both chosen to grow a garden that is exactly 40 feet by 60 feet (~12 x 18 meters).

37 permies.com/t/36537 (giant hugelkultur)

Here is the amount of effort Bob puts into his conventional garden in the fifth year:

Task	Hours
Starting plants indoors	6
Finding a manure source, getting a load of manure and spreading it	5
Tilling in the manure (plus tiller maintenance)	3
Planting seeds and transplanting	5
Weeding	30
Fertilizing	8
Irrigating	45
Controlling pests	8
Cleaning up in the fall	4
Total	114

Here is the amount of effort Alice puts into her permaculture garden in the fifth year:

Task	Hours
Planting seeds	2
Adding mulch (from other parts of the property to garden)	3
Doing chop-and-drop mulching	3
Total	10

That's 114 hours for Bob's conventional garden and 10 hours for Alice's permaculture garden. Alice *is* putting in less than one tenth of the effort of Bob!

In addition, the permaculture garden produces twice as much food because:

- It has steep hugelkultur beds, which nearly double the growing space.

- It's full of aged soil with a five-year-old mycelium network.

- The conventional garden has exposed soil between plants and between rows of plants – about 50% of the garden is exposed soil; the permaculture garden grows food so intensively that there is hardly any exposed soil.

- Most plants produce more with half-day sun than with full sun.

- Perennials grow taller – growing food higher up, off the ground, in combination with foods grown on the ground.

- Mulch and polyculture have been proven to produce bigger plants, producing far larger harvest.

- There is lower pest and disease pressure.

- The extended growing season gives plants more time to produce more food.

As just a touch of frosting on the cake: maybe you can start to save your own seeds. And put some small effort into selecting seeds for the plants that did the very best on your soil, in your climate and with your style of irrigation, to double your overall production again![38]

38 permies.com/t/31939 (seed selection)

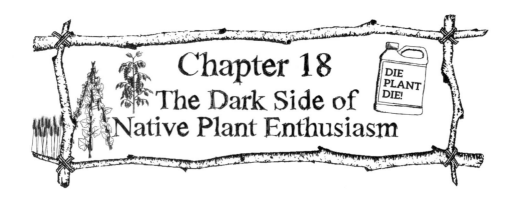

Chapter 18
The Dark Side of Native Plant Enthusiasm

Over the last few decades, I have met a lot of very lovely people who are freaky enthusiastic about native plants.[1] As much as they seem to powerfully advocate a positive thing, I must confess that I have now been down this road so many times that, when I encounter somebody advocating native plants, my stomach twists into a knot. I often choose to change the subject in an effort to keep the conversation friendly.

When I first heard of arguments about native plants, I could not comprehend how there could possibly be anything to argue over. If there are such strong advocates for native plants, it seems that there must be another group that is against native plants. How can anybody advocate against native plants? It turns out that nobody is doing that. It's just that the "pro native plant" campaigns wish to kill the competition. Not just on their property, but on all property.

I think the argument for native plants (or, more accurately, *against* non-native plants) is that there used to be all these different spots with interesting stuff growing. With international travel and trade, seeds have been introduced from all over the world such that all places everywhere are losing their botanic distinctiveness. The corollary to that is that a lot of species that used to do well here are being crowded out by species that do even better here.

Native to When?

It is my impression that here in Montana, a plant is considered "native" if it was growing here before white people showed up. Although there were some white people popping in around 1743, it seems that we draw the line at 1804, when Lewis and Clark came through. Native Americans moved a lot of seeds around before white folks got here with their seeds, but I'm willing to let this go when selecting the official native plant date.

I suppose the passion for native plants could be a sort of guilt thing: white people brought a bunch of seeds here, and those plants are overwhelming the plants that were already here such that the cool plants that were here before could go extinct without a bit of intervention.

A lot of folks want to repair the problems caused by their ancestors, so a date is selected. Everything before that date is "native" and things that showed up after that date are "non-native." Crisp and clear.

1 permies.com/t/41008 (native plants)

Of course, there were plants that showed up before 1743 that were invasive and a nuisance. A great example is the Douglas fir tree.[2] White people looooove the Douglas fir tree. It's great for building stuff we like to build. The folks who were living here before 1743 didn't care for it. They would burn it out. It kept trying to take over land that was growing food. Oh, sure, they found uses for it, but they also worked to get rid of it in spaces where it was a bother. Maybe there have been some people who think that the date for "native" should have been before the Douglas fir tree showed up.

Past Invasives Are Now "Native." When Will Current Invasives Become "Native"?

At one point in time, there were no Douglas fir trees. Then they showed up and sort of wiped out lots of other species of cool stuff. Now they are labeled "native." No white people involved. There are similar stories for nearly all plants. Species come and species go. Survival of the fittest. Granted, when human beings with their fancy boats and explorer boots came along, this whole process was dramatically accelerated.

I want to do a bit of a mental exercise: I want to embrace the spirit of the native-plants movement and look at what plants are here today that would have made it here even if the whole white-people-acceleration thing didn't happen. After all, this whole succession thing is happening all the time. Birds and other critters help. Wind can carry seeds dozens or hundreds of miles. And the Native American people spread seeds – accidentally and on purpose!

Maybe half the plants that are currently being sprayed because they are deemed non-native would get a note from Science saying something like "Please don't kill dandelions anymore, we decided that they would have made it here by now due to wind and birds and Native American people. So we added it to the 'native' list. Thanks!"

The Shifting Definitions of "Noxious Weeds"

The concept of the "noxious weed" started with the idea of plants that could be toxic to farm animals. Animals know instinctively to avoid these plants, but if you fence an animal in, and they run out of good food, they will experiment with whatever plants are left. As long as your animals have plenty of food, there is little value in removing "noxious weeds."

The term "noxious weeds" was adopted by the government and expanded to include any plant that somebody found annoying, even native plants. Usually, they are volunteer plants that do better than the planted monocrop. The theory is that if you claim a plant is threatening your crops, you can make the plant illegal. Then you obliterate it, force your neighbors to obliterate it, and then it won't be a problem anymore. In theory. That said, some seeds will wait in the soil for a hundred years before germinating…

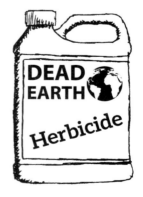

Lots and lots of people have added their favorite pet-peeve plants to the list. I once read a list of plants that were a mix of "noxious weeds" and other plants that are legally required to be eliminated. As I read the list, I recognized nearly half of the plants as extremely beneficial permaculture plants.

2 permies.com/t/4770 (Douglas fir)

Lipstick on a Pig: Native Plant Organizations and Herbicide Companies

Herbicides are generally recognized as the best way to get rid of unwanted plants. A lot of native-plant organizations receive a lot of love (in the form of actual dollars) from herbicide companies. Weed boards also get a lot of support from herbicide companies. The laws against weeds are often lobbied for by herbicide companies. Granted there are exceptions, but as a general rule of thumb, this is the case.

I know that whenever I hear of a native-plant organization, my first thought is "funded by herbicide companies" or "lipstick on an herbicide company." The same goes for weed boards – just looking for an excuse to spray some product. The weird thing is that a lot of these organizations are nonprofit organizations.

They love the Earth by poisoning it.

Getting rid of the non-native plants is a huge task. Billions of dollars? Trillions? It isn't something that you would just do one time. It would be something where it would be a massive task and then it would take that much again every ten years to maintain it. It will never end, but as long as the war wages on, herbicide companies will keep making money.

Myth: Native Plants Will Perform Better in Your Area

If this were true, why do we have any concern over non-native plants threatening native plants?

Native-Plant Enthusiasts Eat Only Native Crops, Right?

I've met some people who are so passionate about native plants that they insist that anything that is non-native should be removed. When I try to ask what percentage of their diet is from native plants… well, it takes a while to get a clear answer, but so far the answer appears to be, nearly universally, less than 1%.

I would like to suggest that people living in town with a quarter of an acre plant a permaculture food system. Native-plant people tend to take that same piece of land and plant 100% native species, which is fine. The problem I have is when they get angry at other folks for not doing the same.

I like to think that if people nurture a permaculture food system on their quarter of an acre, they might, someday, be able to grow half of the food that they eat. I think that this might save two acres of farmland that would otherwise need to grow their food. That two acres could be left as wild land which, hopefully, will include a lot of native plants.

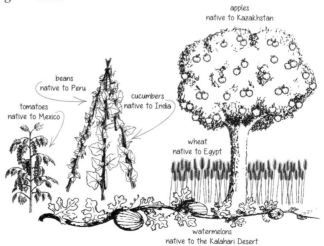

apples
native to Kazakhstan

beans
native to Peru

cucumbers
native to India

tomatoes
native to Mexico

wheat
native to Egypt

watermelons
native to the Kalahari Desert

One Person Managing 20,000 Acres vs One Person Managing 10 Acres

I've heard that the majestic Russian olive tree is no longer allowed to be sold in Montana. There is concern that it is displacing native plants. My impression is that it is growing in places that are nearly devoid of any plant life, and it basically creates an oasis so other plants (including natives) can get started.

I have talked to three plant experts who are certain that it is good to put Russian olive on the noxious list, but I never did understand what the downside is – other than "it is not a native plant." I talked to six other plant experts and they seemed to be confused as well.

My thinking goes like this: It is a tree. If you don't like it, a chainsaw will fix your problem. It's not like the tree will run away while you are chasing it with a chainsaw.

This makes me think that there are some people who are powerful advocates of native plants AND they own 20,000 acres (~8000 hectares) AND they have paid some enormous amount of money to cut down the Russian olives (because they are not native) and the Russian olive trees come back. So, naturally, they want to make sure there are no Russian olive trees growing within a hundred miles so that they might possibly be able to reduce their non-native-tree-cutting budget. After all, if you are one person with ten acres (~4 hectares) and you don't like Russian olive trees, you can cut them down pretty quickly. You can use the wood for firewood or make a hugelkultur bed for other plants.

The Pow Wow Grounds in Elmo, Montana

I was once invited to the Pow Wow Grounds in Elmo, Montana, to give permaculture advice. While giving my advice, they told me that they had received advice from a native-plants person – the suggestion was, of course, all native plants. I told them I thought that would certainly be interesting. I told them that, because of all the work involved, the cost for all native plants would be about 1.1 million dollars to set up and $200,000 per year to maintain.

I then proposed that they do permaculture on most of the property and have a small area that would be established and maintained as "common plants growing in this area in 1804." This plan would cost about one tenth of the all-native plan to implement, and it would cost nearly nothing to maintain.

I went on to point out that when mullein came to the area, the Native Americans found 17 different uses for this plant.[3] I would think that, for all the plants that arrived through the centuries, Native Americans found uses and found a way to live with the changes. It would seem that Native Americans embrace all of nature and do not exercise a bigotry based on some arbitrary date. For the record, my philosophy appeared to be well embraced.

3 permies.com/t/mullein

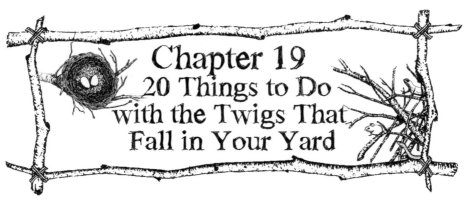

Chapter 19
20 Things to Do with the Twigs That Fall in Your Yard

Some people fill 12 or more green bins in a year with the twigs and branches that fall in their yard. If you are someone with very few twigs in your yard, I would totally understand if you want to just skip ahead to the next chapter.

I am mystified by people who put their twigs on the curb or rent an obnoxious, loud, petroleum-powered, smelly (not to mention dangerous) chipper. Keep those branches, twigs, rotten logs, and Christmas trees![1] That stuff is gardener's gold! Here is a quick list of twenty things that can be done with that wood, keeping it on your property, and not having to fool with a wood-eating, fire-breathing monster named "Chipper":[2]

1. Make your own mulch. A huge branch can be reduced to flat mulch in about one minute with a pruner. I usually clip at the bends in the twigs and branches – every foot or so. A huge pile of branches and twigs will become about 30 times smaller in 15 minutes. Using that branch as mulch helps to work the organic matter into the soil before it goes up into the atmosphere.

2. Cover it in soil to make hugelkultur beds.[3] This is best with the logs (green logs work too) and thick branches. This is an excellent use for a stump – no need to pull it or grind it, just cover it with soil.

3. In Finland, they use small branches and twigs between muddy spots and the house. You can make a muddy spot less muddy, or you can create a place near the house to wipe your feet.[4] When the twigs decompose in the spring, it feeds the soil.

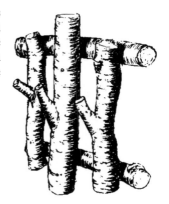

1 permies.com/t/61382 (Christmas trees)
2 permies.com/p/539940 (chipper advice)
3 permies.com/t/hugelkultur
4 permies.com/t/11925 (tree mat)

4. Put the wood in a dry place[5] for a while and then use it for firewood. With a rocket mass heater,[6] a rocket cook stove,[7] or a rocket oven,[8] the trimmings from a small yard may meet all of your fuel needs for the rest of your life.

5. Create butterfly, bird, and other wildlife habitats by making a brush pile. Many gardeners report a dramatic reduction in pest problems by adding a few brush piles near their gardens.[9] Without the brush piles it looks tidier, but then you must do the work that nature would have done for you.

6. With a bit of jute, it's a snap to make a twig trellis or arbor for your garden.[10] Usually, in about ten minutes. And, when they get old, you can mulch the branches and the jute together.

7. Make a junk pole fence[11] – this could be the difference between raising a garden for your family and feeding the local deer.

8. If you have some woodshop skills, you can make chairs,[12] furniture,[13] name tags, coasters, bird houses,[14] benches,[15] planter boxes, tool handles,[16] coat racks,[17] and much, much more. If the wood is fresh black locust wood,[18] whatever you do with it will last about ten times longer outdoors than cedar without adding a drop of paint or stain.

9. Make garden stakes.

10. Throwing branches and logs into ponds will usually reduce algae problems and give fish and amphibians a place to hide from predators.

11. Make roasting sticks for marshmallows, hotdogs, and the like!

12. Make tomato cages.

13. Build a chinampa[19] – the most fertile growing system ever developed (that we know of) – which is simply a pile of brush put into the water at the edge of a pond. Eventually the brush gets compacted enough that you can add some soil.

14. Innoculate logs to grow mushrooms.

---

5 permies.com/t/31987 (wood shed)
6 permies.com/t/41635 (rocket mass heaters)
7 permies.com/t/72880 (rocket cook stove)
8 permies.com/t/86578 (rocket ovens)
9 permies.com/t/108865 (brush piles)
10 permies.com/t/761 (trellis)
11 permies.com/t/47946 (junk pole fence)
12 permies.com/t/1239 (chairs from logs)
13 permies.com/t/25503 (roundwood furniture)
14 permies.com/t/74392 (bird houses)
15 permies.com/t/51646 (benches)
16 permies.com/t/16956 (axe handles)
17 permies.com/t/61361 (coat racks)
18 permies.com/t/4078 (black locust)
19 permies.com/p/9496 (chinampas)

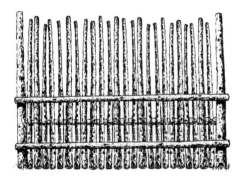

15. Smoke foods if you have the right species of twigs.[20]

16. Make deer deterrent.[21]

17. Make wattle fencing.[22]

18. If the sticks are bigger than you want, let some goats and hogs have them for a week – they will get smaller quickly.

19. Mill lumber.[23] Yes, this requires a lot of big logs.

20. Build all sorts of structures from poles and logs.[24]

This list is not exhaustive. There are lots of other cool things you can do with sticks and branches. This is just one more example of how, when we spend more than five seconds to solve a problem, all sorts of neat ideas pop up.[25] In addition, most of the time one pound of tree works out to be pretty close to one pound of carbon dioxide.[26] With some of these techniques you are effectively sequestering your own carbon! It would be yet another step toward your own personal carbon neutrality.

If you live on acreage, we can triple this list, as a person can develop a powerful symbiotic relationship with a woodland.[27]

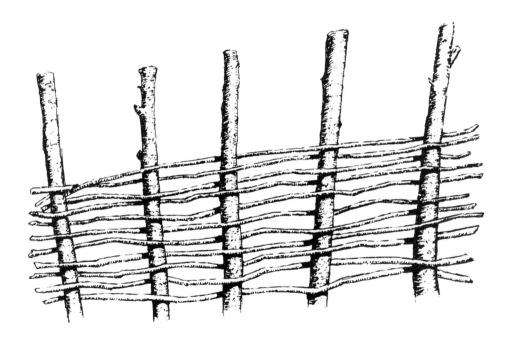

20 permies.com/t/108866 (smoking woods)
21 permies.com/t/93119 (deer deterrent)
22 permies.com/t/51485 (wattle fencing)
23 permies.com/t/28678 (electric sawmill)
24 permies.com/t/47740 (skiddable structures)
25 permies.com/p/540560 (more wood uses)
26 permies.com/t/108857 (tree CO_2 conversion)
27 permies.com/t/43243 (*The Woodland Way*)

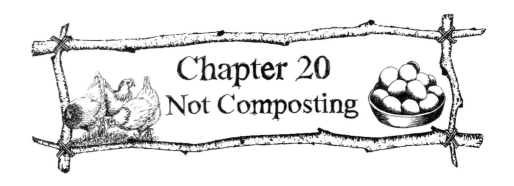

Chapter 20
Not Composting

Gardeners all over the world are intoxicated, with stars in their eyes, over the nearly magical properties of homemade compost. And they are 100% correct. Homemade compost gives any gardener superpowers (by the way, I am talking about homemade compost and not the industrial waste sold as "compost").

But…I think most gardeners are basking in the glow of the upsides and have not really contemplated the downsides.[1] I wish to draw attention to the downsides and then paint a picture that includes all of the upsides, while dodging nearly all of the downsides.

When I did my master gardener training with Helen Atthowe[2] in 1996, I was fortunate to see her amazing composting operation. It was hundreds of feet long and about six feet tall. I had done a lot of composting by then, but I learned that her compost was ten times better than mine and in far greater quantity. She had written a fat book on very advanced stuff in the world of composting. In time, we each came to the same conclusion: stop composting.

Composting is easy. Put a bunch of organic matter into a pile. Composting happens. The result is a bunch of organic matter that is as little as 10% the size of the original pile.[3] Where did the other 90% go? Well, there was some water, but most of it went up as nitrogen or carbon into the atmosphere. Wait! Aren't nitrogen and carbon the very things that we are desperately trying to get into our soil?

Another reason I stopped composting is because of the animals. When I switched to portable shelters, I no longer mucked out shelters — so I no longer had that material to add to the compost pile.[4] And, if I feed kitchen scraps to the chickens and pigs, there is just nothing left to compost.

A lot of people import a LOT of organic matter for their composting, and there is a long list of problems with that. One reason is that imported materials almost always contain persistent herbicides in some way, shape, or form.[5] There is also the

the incredible shrinking compost pile

| carbon & nitrogen escaping into the atmosphere | 1 year later |

1 permies.com/t/43333 (composting downsides)
2 permies.com/t/2230 (Helen Atthowe)
3 permies.com/t/107725 (compost shrinkage)
4 permies.com/t/47725 (goat shelter)
5 permies.com/t/57773 (persistent herbicides)

question of "If we all do it, is there going to be enough for everybody? For even a few people? What is the petroleum footprint of moving it? How much work is there in getting it into and out of the truck? Are there any other toxins in those imports that I won't find out about until my growies are sad?"

Turning compost is a lot of work, and, as I may have previously mentioned, I am super lazy. I imagine that the thought of managing a big compost pile turns a lot of people off gardening who otherwise may have found it lovely. I'd rather just not. Then the question becomes "how do we get that carbon and nitrogen into our soil if we don't compost?" There are many ways. My favorite is to feed a lot of that to chickens and pigs. Beyond that, I like Ruth Stout's method of throwing compostables under your garden mulch (but not too close to plants). From there the little critters have a chance at incorporating it into the soil before it goes up into the atmosphere. In some cases (maybe you are infested with raccoons?), it may be worth a little bit of extra work to dig a small hole and bury your compostables in the garden. Let's keep that carbon in the soil.

Composting is great. I just think the above alternatives are better. Much better.

Chapter 21
Better Than Solar Panels: A Solar Food Dehydrator

Long before the refrigerator, freezer, or the art of canning, there was the art of drying food. Even today, people will still put fresh food, in just the right way, on a rock in the sun and end up with a bit of food that can be stored for years. If we optimize this process a bit, we can have food that lasts longer, tastes better, and we can be certain that critters didn't "enhance it" when we weren't looking.

My friend, Mark, has a massive solar food dehydrator. When he first showed it to me, he said that one year a friend gave him a few boxes of plums, so he used a collection of electric food dehydrators to preserve the plums. His electric bill was so ridiculously huge that he could have bought more dried plums than he had received for "free"!

So, Mark built a solar food dehydrator using the "down draft" style. Food dries quickly and without any electricity. The materials cost is paid back in next to no time.

Over the years, there have been many designs for solar dehydrators. The key component is a solar collector where air is warmed and then pushed into a dark box that holds the food on removable trays. The air intake has a screen to keep critters and bugs out. The warm air is pushed through the food, picks up moisture, and leaves the food dry. An excellent solar dehydrator will dry food in a day or less. There are dozens of general designs,[1] and, in the world of trial and error, the "down draft" style has, so far, been the best.[2]

My Quick Tips for Making a "Down Draft" Solar Food Dehydrator

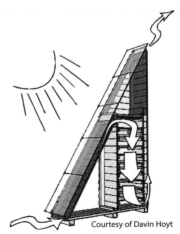

- stainless steel mesh for the food trays

- make the angle of the glass steeper than 45° – use something more like 60°. We are trying to create a thermosiphon and thermosiphons tend to peter out at 45°

- shower door glass does not block some parts of the spectrum like most windows – more spectrum means more heat

- don't use treated wood, plywood, waferboard,

Courtesy of Davin Hoyt

1 permies.com/t/762 (food dehydrators)
2 permies.com/t/74059 (dehydrator plans)

or anything that has glues in it – instead, build it in such a way that all wood needs no paint other than "the black" for collecting solar heat

- make your own paint for the solar collector "black"[3]

A Natural Recipe for Solar Dehydrator "Black"

1. Take 2 gallons (~8 liters) of skim milk.
2. Add 2 cups (~500 milliliters) of white vinegar, apple cider vinegar, or lemon juice.
3. Let it sit for 2 hours up to overnight. This will curdle the milk.
4. Moisten ½ cup (~120 milliliters) of type S hydrated lime with water until it reaches a thick, pasty consistency.
5. Strain the milk curds.
6. Combine the curds with the lime to make the paint base.
7. Mix one part paint base with one to three parts powdered charcoal.

Ta-da! Solar dehydrator "black!"

A Few Things You Can Do with a Solar Dehydrator

Properly dehydrated food can last several years and is compact and light. Some dehydrated foods can be powdered, and some dehydrated foods are considered better (tastier) than the original fresh food.

Here are a few of the many things you can make with a solar dehydrator:[4]

- Dried fruit (pretty much candy)
- Jerky (the meat version of candy)
- Dried herbs
- Cookies
- Crackers
- Dried sprouts
- Squash flour (good for baking)
- Sauces dried into sauce leather
- Dried mushrooms
- Energy bars
- Dried flowers

With nothing more than a garden and a solar dehydrator, we can dramatically reduce our relationship with commercial ag systems that have such significant petroleum, carbon, and TFD footprints. And with a magnificent garden and a good solar dehydrator, we could be adding a lot of luxury to our lives along the way.

3 permies.com/p/574818 (natural paint)
4 permies.com/t/85784 (dehydrator uses)

Chapter 22
Breaking the
Toxic Water Cycle with
Greywater Recycling

All sorts of toxic waste are regularly dumped into sewage treatment systems by industries and homeowners alike – either legally or illegally. That stuff can do all sorts of funky things to the natural world and is often not something that the treatment plants can properly handle – so it goes into the river. On top of that, in some places, people have decided to seize the opportunity to take the chunky stuff from the sewage treatment plant and make money by turning it into commercial compost! Now it's not just in the river – you can spread the toxic waste on your garden too![1]

If 80% of people would reduce how much they sent to the sewage treatment plant by something like 90%, the concentration of toxins in the system would be greater, thus exposing serious problems so they can be more directly addressed. Plus you'd likely pay less taxes for sewage treatment systems.

If you have a septic tank and a drain field, this chapter is relevant to you too. These systems are least efficient when there is a lot of water going through them. And an inefficient system means that some of the toxicity could be leaching into the groundwater directly below your drain field. Depending on your situation, you could be pulling that toxicity right back up with your well pump. Oops.

So, the goal is to reduce wastewater. And by reducing wastewater we are effectively making the world less toxic by taking action in our own backyard.[2]

Water in your home effectively exists in one of three forms: whitewater, blackwater, or greywater. Whitewater is the stuff you can drink, blackwater has poop in it, and greywater is the water that comes from your sinks, tubs, showers, and laundry. Urine can also be considered greywater, though some people prefer to lump it in with blackwater instead.

The current system used by most homes is to mix greywater and blackwater together and feed it to a septic tank or a sewage treatment plant. Blackwater might contain pathogens, so it needs careful treatment to prevent spreading illness. On the other hand, greywater is a hundred times easier to deal with than blackwater. If we mix the two together, then it all becomes blackwater. But, by keeping them separate and recycling the greywater for other purposes, we can reduce the amount of blackwater that needs treatment.

It is worth noting that people are far more open to using toxic gick if they are going to simply rinse away the toxins and send it all to the mysterious and magical

1 permies.com/t/98615 (sewage compost)
2 permies.com/t/72483 (greywater systems)

land of NIMBY (Not In My Back Yard). Paint residue, turpentine, powerful cleaners, bleach...if this is going into a greenhouse full of beautiful plants, you might not be so quick to use these things – thus reducing your toxic footprint even further.

There are many different styles of systems you can use in your home to reduce wastewater, recycle greywater, and reduce your toxic footprint. Here are eight levels of wastewater reduction for you to consider, depending on how much you want to do:

> **Level 1:** Dishpans and buckets. Grab some greywater and reuse it so there is a reduction in water use and treatment systems can work better.
>
> **Level 2:** A small plumbing modification for one greywater system – typically laundry.
>
> **Level 3:** Most greywater is reused in some form seasonally.
>
> **Level 3.5:** Most greywater is reused year round.
>
> **Level 4:** All greywater is reused year round.
>
> **Level 4.5:** All greywater and blackwater is reused year round.
>
> **Level 5:** All greywater and blackwater is reused year round and nearly all toxins going into these systems are eliminated.
>
> **Level 5.5:** All greywater and blackwater is reused year round and all toxins going into these systems are eliminated.

In my opinion, the best resource available for greywater treatment systems is Art Ludwig's excellent book *Create an Oasis with Greywater*.[3] In his book, Art describes a number of different systems, how to install them properly, how to please the building inspector, and more. There's no way I could do Art's book justice here, but I will bring up a few ideas to give you a picture of what's possible.

A Quickie Greywater System

Most people let a lot of water flow down the drain just waiting for the water to warm up. The cheapest and easiest greywater system that pretty much anyone can use regardless of where they live is the bucket system.[4]

The bucket system is simple. All you have to do is put a bucket in the sink or in the shower to catch the water that is usually wasted while you wait for warm water to arrive. In my house we also use a dishpan in the sink when we do the dishes, using minimal dish soap and opting for hot water to clean our dishes instead.[5]

The water in the bucket is used for things like watering houseplants or flushing the toilet (especially if the toilet was presented with...um...too much of a challenge?). This technique does require manually emptying the bucket (it's pretty much free, what did you expect?), but it also helps one be aware of the amount of water they are using and provides a good incentive to reduce it.

3 permies.com/t/43124 (Art Ludwig)
4 permies.com/t/89452 (bucket system)
5 permies.com/t/18221 (minimal soap)

Building a Simple Greywater System

A step up from the lifehack greywater system would be to install what Art Ludwig calls a "laundry-to-landscape system."[6] As the title suggests, this system takes the water coming out of your washing machine and uses it for irrigation in your yard.

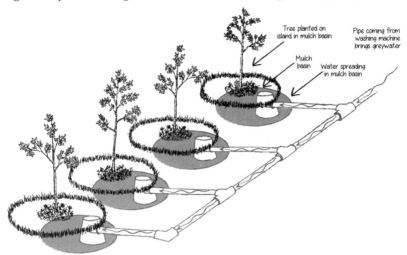

Tree planted on island in mulch basin
Pipe coming from washing machine brings greywater
Mulch basin
Water spreading in mulch basin

These systems are not complicated and are quite effective. The system relies on the pump in the washing machine to distribute the greywater out to a system of branched drains that lead into mulch basins in your yard. The mulch holds the moisture in place where it is taken up by a tree that grows on an island in the middle of the basin. For cold climates it is possible to set up such a system to include a diverter valve so that in the winter the water can be sent to the sewer or septic system instead.

Note that plants and soil organisms don't like most laundry detergents, let alone bleach. It's important to consider what you're putting in your laundry machine.

Cold Climate Greywater Systems

For those who live where it gets really cold, sending a whole bunch of greywater outside to be frozen in the winter is asking for trouble.[7] Once it warms up, there would be 4-6 months of accumulated greywater that suddenly needs processing. This overloads the system and things start to get funky. The idea is for greywater systems to be safe, positive influences in recycling our water for increased benefit in the landscape – so please don't do that.

If you live in a cold climate and want to harvest all of your greywater year round, you probably need to consider some kind of system where the greywater is processed inside a greenhouse.[8] A nice thing about such a system is that most greywater is quite warm, so you're helping to heat the greenhouse at the same time! And you're getting access to water inside your greenhouse during a season where rainwater capture may not be possible – so it's a twofer.

The one thing I would like to add here is that if you are thinking about edibles

6 permies.com/t/1832 (laundry to landscape)
7 permies.com/t/52076 (cold climate greywater)
8 permies.com/t/51950 (greywater greenhouse)

in such a system, please make a bigger greenhouse, so that the water can first be thoroughly filtered by things you don't eat.

Becoming a Certified Environmentalist

The plants that are in your greywater system are judging you every day. If you're good at this, they're going to thrive. And if anyone puts anything toxic down the drain, it's going to kill everything.

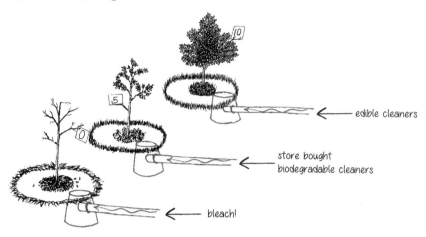

← edible cleaners

← store bought biodegradable cleaners

← bleach!

Reaching wastewater reduction level 5.5 is a serious commitment to living a better life. Suddenly the question becomes "How do you live a life where everything on the other end of that pipe could die based on your decisions on this side of the pipe?" And not only does this affect you, but your visitors too.

Suddenly, toxic household cleaners are no longer an option. Nor are toxic body products. And when you go to paint something, now you're thinking that you're going to have to clean that brush afterward. You start to contemplate whether you can get a paint that doesn't have these problems, and then you even start to contemplate whether that item really needs any paint at all.

Once you get to the point where you are trying to support life out there with what comes out of your plumbing system, congratulations! You are truly owning your own shit!

I think if someone does this and their growies survive for two years without incident, they should be formally recognized by their community. Perhaps they could become a certified environmentalist and get a medal! And when someone isn't sure what to do about an environmental issue, they'd call up a certified environmentalist for their opinion on the matter. Through this, more and more people would start to make positive change and dramatically reduce their toxic footprint.

CERTIFIED ENVIRONMENTALIST

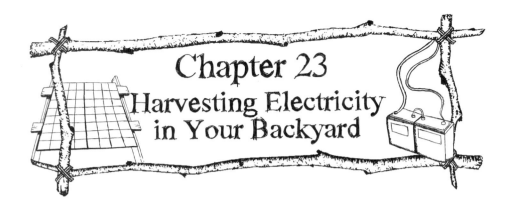

Chapter 23
Harvesting Electricity in Your Backyard

When it comes to clean energy, a lot of people love to blindly say "solar power!" as if the government should just choose solar and then it's all over and all of the energy problems are solved.

We have been told who the villains and heroes of grid power are, and I wish to clearly muddy the waters. Everything on the other end of the wire is nasty – including solar. Here is a brief rogues' gallery:

- **nuclear:** the waste, the dangers, the fuel for war stuff...we are very familiar with a lot of the downsides here. There have been dramatic improvements, and there is talk of the potential of further optimizations.[1] But there are downsides that most people are not aware of (like the waste needs 10,000 years of professional babysitting). And as much as nuclear is a mess, until demand drops, power companies will use whatever is the cheapest in the short run.[2] And there is some thought to public safety – so as much as nuclear seems to be "the worst," it turns out that the death count with nuclear energy is officially less than 200 people, although there is information that suggests numbers approaching an all-time count of one million people. Coal, meanwhile, is casually racking up several million per year.[3]

- **coal:** the worst of the lot in my opinion. Instead of trying to carefully store dangerous waste as with nuclear, coal plants just pump it up into the atmosphere! And even if you go to the most remote wilderness and catch a fish, it's going to be loaded with toxic levels of mercury that came from coal plants.

- **hydro:** the cement has a massive carbon footprint. Plus, each dam obliterates 95% or more of the river wildlife. There is now less than 5% of the salmon remaining than used to be in the rivers in the Pacific Northwest thanks to hydro power, and we artificially

1 permies.com/t/105499 (nuclear optimizations)
2 permies.com/t/108872 (cheapest power)
3 permies.com/t/108874 (energy deaths)

augment the salmon population – what about all the other species? And many dams are on the edge of ceasing to function due to silt building up behind them.

- **wind:** it takes quite a bit of cement to anchor those giant towers. But, compared to the others, wind power is now virtually problem free – and still getting better. The biggest practical problem is pretty obvious: energy demand might be at odds with how much the wind blows – so wind power needs to be augmented by something that has more problems.

- **solar:** the poster child we turn to for "better." Unfortunately, toxic materials are involved in the manufacturing process and in the panels themselves. I hope that by standing up now and expressing "I am worried about the toxicity," we might see optimizations on that front. Additionally, today's panels have a lifespan of about 25 years. Hopefully that will improve as well. But solar still has the same problem as wind: energy demand might go unsatisfied, depending on how much the sun is shining…especially at night. So solar power also needs to be augmented by something else.

Now that we've given all the bigs a quick kick, let's contemplate making our own electricity. Not so much because you are about to make this leap tomorrow, but for the sake of trying on some ideas. To see how this frame of mind looks on you. And to contemplate a richer life that happens to use less energy, from a different angle than we have talked about so far.

I think the best off-grid power source is micro hydro, which often has a negligible environmental footprint.[4] Lots of power, day and night. No silt issues. No massive concrete footprint. Not a lot of parts – so not a lot of bound-up toxicity. It is far better than any other option – but it is often illegal and requires you to have a backyard stream…which most people don't.

While wind is a great champion for on-grid power, it also requires a lot of dedicated people to maintain those moving parts. Smaller-scale systems need that same level of maintenance, and parts will wear out. And the smaller stuff doesn't get high enough to harvest the best wind.[5] Overall, small-scale wind has not been a popular solution. That said, I think there is a lot of room for optimization, so I am grateful to the folks who continue to invest in this space!

Before rolling out my favorite strategy for backyard solar, we first have to get past off-grid's dirty little secret…

Nearly everybody that is off-grid uses propane – which always struck me as a bit odd. It's not like you wander out in the woods to harvest the wild propane, bring it home, and stuff it into your water heater. Propane is part of "the grid." So when people shop around for solar power systems, they see the price tags for a 5 kilowatt system and get sticker shock "WHAT! That's WAY too expensive!" But it gets worse: that system doesn't include heat, hot water, cooking, or a clothes dryer – all of those things will be run on propane. If we choose to skip propane then we are looking at a 20 kW system.

When you are looking at spending over $25,000 for a system that will barely meet your needs for the next ten years, you start to appreciate the low price of the grid and how luxuriant your life is with so much cheap electricity – as long as you don't think about the environmental disaster on the other end of the wire. Therefore, this chapter is about approaching this issue from a different direction.

4 permies.com/t/108876 (micro hydro)
5 permies.com/t/5663 (micro wind)

My friend, Helen Atthowe,[6] spent a few years living in a cabin. At first, she was without power. After a few months, she got the very best solar system I had ever seen: two 135 watt panels, two batteries, and two inverters.[7] Here are the most profound points to this system:

- Because Helen found a comfortable path using much less energy, her system ended up far simpler and easier to work with. As an engineer, one of my favorite "design pearls" is: the fastest and most reliable components of any system are those that are not there.

- Two inverters. One is 2000 watts and one is 400 watts (personally, I would prefer a 3000/200 combo). The larger inverter is turned on for 2 to 3 hours each week and the smaller inverter is turned on for 8 to 12 hours each week. All other energy use is with 12 volt DC power. Solar experts are quick to point out that the amount of power that an inverter uses is very small compared to the amount of power that can be used through it. But my experience is that if you leave the inverter on all the time without using power for anything else, you can end up (in the winter) with no power left for anything else. So use the inverter only when you need it.

Most people who go off-grid suffer without their clothes dryer,[8] hair dryer, air conditioner,[9] etc. Unless, of course, their off-grid situation has the 20,000 watts of solar panels. I would like to suggest that people first explore reducing their energy consumption by 90% while still on the grid, and then they are ready to explore going off-grid.

Rather than a gradual reduction of use, Helen made a leap to zero electrical use for a few months. And then she added in a beautiful, small solar system. This is not the path for everybody, but it is a lovely path to contemplate.

There are a lot of great things to say about moving to solar. And enthusiasm often masks certain downsides, like the toxic footprint. One way to reduce the toxicity by 90% is to reduce the panel count by 90%. And the first step is to contemplate a luxuriant strategy with less electricity.

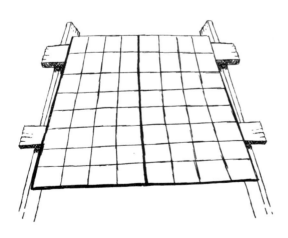
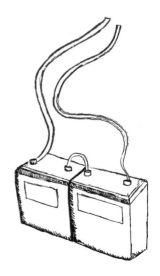

6 permies.com/t/2230 (Helen Atthowe)
7 permies.com/t/85774 (solar system)
8 permies.com/t/dryer
9 permies.com/t/14038 (home cooling)

Chapter 24
The Conventional Lawn
vs a Mowable Meadow

FEAR THE DANDELION! FEAR IT! (wild, psychotic screaming goes here) No, don't fear it. That's just silly.

The amount of money spent to teach you to fear dandelions is huge. All because most people can be convinced to buy dandelion poison. On the opposite end of the spectrum, there is a large movement to replace all lawns with gardens. Although I am bonkers about gardens, I do enjoy a lovely lawn.[1] It's a place for picnics, lounging, yard sales, kids to play, people to gather – it is a huge tool in the community-building tool set.

And I enjoy a lawn tapestry richer than the grass monocrop. I want to add in fifty species of plants and relabel my lawn as a "mowable meadow."[2] And embrace (and eat!) the dandelion. But that's a lovely conversation for five years into the future. For now, let's talk about how to have the most magnificent lawn on your block, without toxic gick, using less water and requiring less effort. Something that will be low in dandelions (and other non-grass plants). And something that will sequester ten times more carbon!

The key to the lawn care game is competition. Make the grass happier than the other plants and have almost nothing but grass.

Battle for the Sun Deathmatch! Rig the Game for Grass!

Mowing high is, by far, the most important thing.[3] By far. Most important. I can say it louder if that will help.

There is a fight for sun. If the grass doesn't shade the dandelion, the dandelion will shade the grass. Sun is food. Food is strength and life. Shade is weakness, disease, and death.

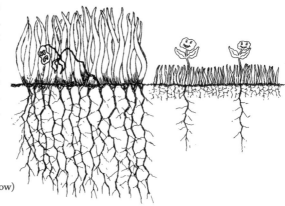

1 permies.com/t/11 (lawn care)
2 permies.com/t/1760 (mowable meadow)
3 permies.com/t/7985 (mowing high)

Grass will shade the dandelion only if it is tall enough. The shade of tall, dense, grass turf will prevent essential light from reaching most dandelions and will aid in the destruction of new baby dandelion seedlings.

MYTH: "If I mow short, it will be longer until I have to mow again." False! Wrong! (SLAP! SLAP! SLAP!) Grass needs grass blades to do photosynthesis (convert sunshine into sugar) to feed the roots. When the blades are whacked off, the grass has to RACE to make more blades to make sugar. It then grows amazingly fast. This fast growth uses up a lot of the grass's stored sugar and weakens the plant. It is now vulnerable to disease and pests! Tall grass is healthier and can use the extra sugar to make rhizomes (more grass plants), thus thickening the turf.

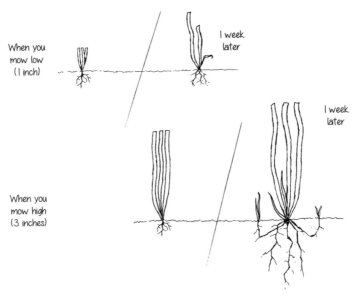

If you have a serious dandelion infestation, consider mowing twice as frequently as you normally do. The sensitive growing point for grass is near the soil. The sensitive growing point for most other plants is near the top of the plant. So when you mow, it's as if you are giving your grass a haircut and cutting the heads off the other plants.

Finally, when mowing, be sure to leave the clippings on the lawn. It adds organic matter and nutrients back into the soil. If you don't leave the clippings, your soil will begin to look more like "dirt" than soil. Soon it will be a form of cement that nothing will grow in and you will have the world's most pitiful lawn. Some people are concerned about grass trimmings "clumping" – that only happens when you mow too short or when you don't mow often enough.

Mowing higher gives the following perks:

- more shade to the soil which leads to less watering
- deeper roots which lead to less watering
- thicker turf which leads to fewer dandelions
- slower vertical growth which leads to less mowing
- more plant matter sequestering carbon

Tough Training Leads to Strong Grasses with Deep, Resilient Roots!

Shallow, frequent watering encourages "thatch." The grass propagates with above-soil runners, like strawberry runners, rather than rhizomes under the soil – there gets to be so many runners that they weave a mat that chokes out water and air. Since the roots are in the top inch or two of soil, a hot day will quickly dry the soil and much of the grass will brown. Dandelion seedlings looooove a daily watering. It's just what they need for a good start.

I recommend watering deeply and less often. This will force your grass roots to go deep into the soil. Deeper than the roots of most other plants. And as the top few inches of soil become bone dry, the seedlings of other plants will die while the grass still enjoys moisture from a little deeper.

Two methods to tell when it is time to water:

- The grass will start to curl before it turns brown. When it starts to curl, that is the best time to water.

- Take a shovel and stick it into the soil about six inches (~15 centimeters). Keep the sun to your left or to your right when you do this – so you can see in the hole. Push the handle forward. If you can see any moisture, wait. If it's all dry, water. If you can't get your shovel to go into the soil this deep, you need more soil.

The first method is the best – especially if you have not yet trained your grass to make deep roots.

A tip for lawn care experts: if it is almost time to water and there is a rain shower – maybe a quarter of an inch (~5 millimeters) – THAT is the best time to water your lawn to give it another three quarters of an inch (~20 millimeters).

Remember, the grass roots are down deep and most weed roots are near the surface. The idea is to keep the top three inches of soil as dry as you can for as long as you can. That quarter of an inch (~5 millimeters) of rain might make it so that your top three inches (~8 centimeters) of soil is well watered but the lower 9 to 20 inches (~20 to 50 centimeters) is on the edge of being pretty dry. This gives the shallow-rooted plants an advantage over your grass!

Another thing about lawn care watering: I have discovered that if you are going to water an inch (~25 millimeters), it is better to water half an inch, wait 90 minutes, and then water another half an inch. Maybe do this once a month. Sometimes when the soil gets really dry, it will repel water. This is called "super deflocculation" (I think Mary Poppins would be impressed with this word!). If you put a little water in first, then wait, the soil is better prepared to take in more water. Remember: water has a strange and powerful attraction to itself. It would much rather stick to itself than disperse through the soil.

Another perk: every time you water, you wash away soil nutrients. So the less you water, the more fertile your soil!

One last point about watering deeply: If your topsoil is only two inches (~5 centimeters) deep, laying down an inch (~2 centimeters) of water is a bad idea. An inch of water is good for watering 12 inches (~30 centimeters) of soil. Further, an inch of water will effectively carry a lot of soil nutrients down deeper. So if your soil is only two inches deep, this rinses away a lot of your soil nutrients! Therefore, deep watering should be done only in conjunction with deep soil.

Deep, Rich, Magnificent Soil vs Thin, Pathetic Dirt

At one place I lived, my soil was only half an inch (~1 centimeter) deep. Even weeds had a tough time growing. Below my half inch of soil were huge river rocks separated by smaller rocks, separated by sand. It bore no resemblance to soil. I added four inches (~10 centimeters) of topsoil. This was done with two dump truck loads at $100 a pop. It covered all of the weeds with enough soil that they could not work through it – and I could start from scratch with my grass seed of choice (I like "tall fescue")!

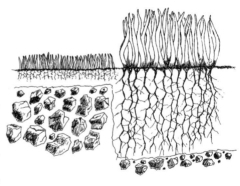

18 inches (~50 centimeters) or more soil would be optimal. I have a friend that has soil this deep. While everyone else waters a dozen times or more over the summer, she waters just once or twice. She uses no fertilizer or pesticides. She has thick, dark-green, weed-free grass. Her lawn is about as "no-brainer lawn care" as you could get.

This is a good time to talk about soil quality too. There is a big difference between dirt and soil.[4] Soil is rich in microbial life and has a lot of organic matter in it. Dirt comes in many forms and it's a challenge to get anything to grow in it. If you are getting "topsoil" delivered to your house, be prepared for it to bear more resemblance to "dirt." Make sure that the source is full of non-grass plants – this is to make sure that it does not contain persistent herbicides. Do not get "soil" that is made from dirt and commercial compost.

Free Fertilizers Stomp the Poopies out of the Commercial Offerings

In 1996, I completed my master gardener training. I ended up being sent to several homes to give advice on a lot of things, and the #1 problem with lawns was that the soil was "deflated." What I mean is that there would be trees in the lawn and there were huge roots exposed. Sometimes the roots protruded six to ten inches (~15 to 25 centimeters) like the tops of giant eels in a river of dirt. The grass would be thin and pitiful in a pathetic, gray dirt that nearly resembled cement. Every time I said the same thing: "When you mow, do you haul away the clippings?" "Yes." "And when the leaves fall off the tree, do you haul the leaves away too?" "Yes." At one point, these people had "soil" that would pump out happy trees and happy grass. Then they took all that lovely organic matter that would have fed the soil and hauled it away. As the years passed, there was less and less organic matter in the soil – until all that was left was pathetic dirt. The soil "deflated" into dirt.

With the help of a few earthworms, this process can be reversed. Lots of organic matter on top of the soil will not only feed the soil at the surface, but earthworms

4 permies.com/t/63914 (dirt & soil)

will take it pretty deep into the soil. The trick is that soil will take in organic matter, but dirt will not. If you set the organic matter on a concrete sidewalk, the concrete doesn't take it in. If you set that same organic matter on the rich soil of a garden, the organic matter will be "consumed" by the soil in a few weeks or months. And just like most garden plants, grass loves a rich soil too.

The simplest thing to do is to mow high and leave your clippings on the lawn. In time, this will work. I have some bigger things you can do, but first, let's understand what grass wants.

Grass is a nitrogen pig. Legumes (such as clover and black medic) can get their nitrogen from the air (remember that the air we breathe is 78% nitrogen!). So, when you see legumes taking over your lawn, you know that your soil is nitrogen-poor. Suppose you have a lawn that is about 50% clover. I think that's pretty great! As long as you leave all of your clippings on the lawn, you will be fine. In three to six years, you will probably get to less than 10% clover. Patience is a powerful tool.

Of course, most people want an amazing lawn instantly. The quick solutions you can buy have varying degrees of toxicity. Rather than explore which villain is the worst, here is a quick list of nontoxic stuff that will work:

- lawn clippings from your mulching mower
- pee on the shortest grasses
- **organic** hay tossed on your lawn just before you mow
- nitrogen-fixing plants in the lawn such as clover or black medic

Long-Term Soil vs Short-Term Fertilizer

Adding high-carbon material to the soil will, in a way, do the opposite of fertilizing the soil. In fact, it will cause "nitrogen immobilization" where most nitrogen in the soil will be temporarily unavailable to the grass. But this adds organic matter to the soil, giving parking places for water and nutrients (including nitrogen) and housing for the microscopic life that inhabits soil. It is that life and the carbon that are the difference between dirt and soil.

High-carbon material you can add to the soil surface of your lawn:

- leaves that have been chopped up by a mulching mower
- organic straw tossed on your lawn just before you mow[5]
- a dusting of sawdust (not woodchips) from untreated wood

If your soil is more like dirt right now, then you might want to go easy on the carbon stuff until your soil is amazing. With that in mind, I suggest…

Bringing in the REAL Professionals (Hint: They Don't Wear Clothes)

You probably don't want to till up your yard. I don't want you to till up your yard. That's a lot of work! And it looks really ugly until the new lawn gets established. The grass you have now is a fine breed of grass – it's just in terrible soil. The mission is to improve the soil so the grass will be happy.

I wish for you to build a dozen or more "worm towns." Dig a hole about three feet (~90 centimeters) deep and at least 8 inches (~20 centimeters) in diameter. Then refill

5 permies.com/t/9191 (hay fertilizer)

the hole with that soil plus all the fixings for the most pampered living for earthworms. About eight inches from the top of the hole, add a half gallon (~2 liters) of magnificent garden soil – try to keep it in a block or sphere. Think of this magnificent garden soil blob as a "seed" containing garden magic (earthworm pods, good bacteria and fungus, soil building seeds, etc.) and if you break "the seed" or spread it out, all the "magic" dies.

As the years pass, your earthworm population will skyrocket. Organic matter will be spread all through the soil. The earthworms will not only create thousands of tiny tunnels allowing air and water better access to the roots of your grasses, but they will create magnificent soil structure. Combined with your efforts of adding organic matter to the surface (maybe with nothing more than what is left behind from the mulching mower), your soil will become excellent and your grass will be strong and healthy – without buying fertilizers.

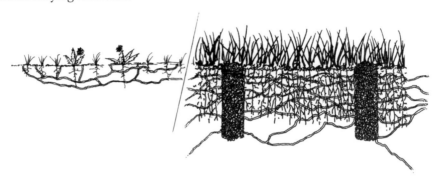

Three feet (~90 centimeters) is not a randomly selected depth. To survive a winter in Montana, earthworms hibernate about three feet deep. But in hard dirt it is challenging for them to get that deep. Worm towns come with an earthworm freeway between the surface and three feet deep – easy peasy!

In time, the packed dirt between each worm town will become indistinguishable from the worm towns. It is as if the worm towns that you created all grew to form one massive, magnificent worm world – all in your yard.

Stuff to put in the hole with your soil:

- kitchen scraps, unwanted plants, or rotting matter
- sticks
- a half gallon of garden soil (keep in a gob – do not mix with other stuff)
- lawn clippings
- a little bit of sawdust (optional)
- a few leaves (optional)

Only do it once. Ever.[6] In other words, this isn't a thing that you have to do every year, or every ten years. Once is enough. After this, just keep putting organic matter on top of the soil and the earthworms will take care of everything from there.

6 permies.com/t/3841 (worm towns)

Part 5

Counter the Footprint of 20 People on a Homestead

Chapter 25
How Vegans Benefit from Caring for Cattle, Chickens, Hogs, Etc.

I met Sepp Holzer[1] in Tacoma, Washington in 2009. I had been studying his work for about nine years at this point and was so excited to meet him in person. After his presentation, somebody asked what he would do about controlling blackberries.[2] In the Tacoma area, untended garden areas quickly become a giant blackberry patch. Sepp said that he would put a strand of electric fence around the blackberries and run hogs in there. A man then said "I'm a vegan, so I don't have pigs. What should I do?" And Sepp said "Then you must do the pig's work. Next question."

The concerns that vegans have are valid. I agree with every concern. And yet, by the end of this chapter, I hope that vegans will choose a life rich with animals while keeping their noble dietary choices.

Not only do I agree with the concerns of the vegans, I have even more concerns − concerns that most vegans have never heard of.

A few of the concerns of vegans:

- tiny cages
- animals standing in their own shit
- disrespectful harvest
- no access to greenery or sun
- carbon footprint

A few of my concerns that most vegans are not aware of:

- medicated feed
- feed that is not what that animal is designed to eat
- lack of feed choice for the animal
- feed that is so bad that it is not allowed to be sold for human consumption
- raised in stench (horrible for the animals and offensive to neighbors)

1 richsoil.com/sepp
2 permies.com/t/6512 (blackberry control)

To have this conversation, I need to start by expressing the following levels of care:

1. factory farms
2. organic factory farms
3. what most people do when raising their own animals
4. setting all the animals free
5. providing a life better than a life in the wild
6. pampering the animals
7. something that would inspire a Disney movie about a little girl and all of her homestead animal friends

I am going to assume that the reader is already cringing at the thought of factory farms. And this might be the first time that the reader learns of "organic" factory farms that are just as bad (if not worse).

But this book is about solving these problems in your backyard. So I desperately need to express that I am incredibly uncomfortable with the way that 99% of people care for their livestock. As an example, I have been to many people's places where they were excited to show me their animal systems. When I got there, I found the animals standing in four inches (10 centimeters) of their own shit. To me, this is cruel and unacceptable. And yet the people said something like: "I must be taking good care of these animals because most of them haven't died."

If we're going to care for animals, I think we need to do much better. The moment you put an animal in a cage or behind a fence, you are taking responsibility for the welfare of that animal. If you are a person of conscience, then you want to treat that animal well – giving it a life better than if it were on its own in the wild. Can we, at the very least, contemplate what it would mean to excessively pamper these animals?[3]

Contemplations in Pampering an Animal

I once visited a farm and the farmer complained to me "Yesterday the chickens got out and wiped out half of our strawberries!" I thought that if any of us only had dirty water and moldy "food" we would want to gorge on those strawberries too.

Suppose you like to eat eggs. Would you rather eat eggs from a chicken that...

- eats from a magnificent garden, or
- is limited to a pen that gets no sun and only has feed that seems unpalatable to you?

3 permies.com/t/64984 (raising animals)

Does your fence define your critter prison, or does it define the safe space to keep predators out? Would a chicken prefer to be inside or outside that fence? With or without strawberries?

Just once, give the chicken the choice between your dinner and theirs. When the chicken prefers their dinner, I think it is safe to say that you are pampering that chicken.[4]

How to Get Five Times More Garden Growth by Gardening with Animals

Bison, deer, elk…all sorts of animals stick together in herds to better protect themselves against predators. A large mob of animals would come to an area, eat, and leave quickly – this was the natural way. And the land would thrive from these visits. At least until we put up so much fence that this was no longer really possible. Land without these visits has been proven to atrophy and turn to desert.[5]

In the last few decades, a few farmers have attempted to emulate this with their pastures, moving animals every few days to the next pasture. The results are freakishly positive. Massive research has been done with this, resulting in about 40 different reasons this happens. There are now dozens of books and hundreds of white papers. But for our needs, all we need is: "It works."

When I give a presentation and touch on paddock shift systems, I ask the audience for validation on this point: "Using paddock shift leads to five times more growies." I usually get four or five people who confirm that they have used paddock shift and this is their observation also. A few people have said it is more than five times.

I am going to define a paddock shift system as a system comprised of at least four fenced paddocks. The general idea is that a group of animals is allowed into a fresh paddock and they all get excited because their favorite food is in there! Once the animals have eaten about 30% of the plants in the paddock, they are moved into the next paddock which has had at least 30 days of rest. That way the animals will be able to pick their favorite foods and not be forced to settle for the plants that are toxic to them.

Whenever folks learn about paddock shift, the next idea is "Why don't I just remove all the toxic plants and then I can leave the animals in the paddock longer?" The answer is: "Because toxic plants are good for animals – sort of." When animals feel sick, suddenly plants that they wouldn't normally eat happen to smell and taste good. The animals, effectively, self-medicate using their instincts as a guide.[6] The key is that we are not forcing the animals to eat these toxic plants.

A quick recipe for upgrading your garden to a garden jungle: divide your garden into at least four paddocks (a dozen paddocks would be better). And then do paddock shift. Make sure that the animals never take more than 30% and make sure that each paddock gets at least 30 days of rest. Presto! Five times more growies! Vegans get more vegan chow by having a symbiotic relationship with animals.

4 richsoil.com/chickens (raising chickens)
5 permies.com/t/71609 (reversing desertification)
6 permies.com/t/1312 (animals self-medicating)

Building Your Soul with a Plethora of Life Instead of Zappity Zap Zap

Most people trying paddock shift for the first time buy an electric fence. Please give me a chance to dissuade you.

An electric fence is not a physical barrier. It is a psychological barrier. The design is such that an animal gets zapped once and will hate that so much that they will never go near the fence again. The heartbreak I have around electric fence is multifaceted:

- **Heartbreak 1:** People implement it poorly. Usually the zap is weak, so the fence doesn't contain the animals, and the animals get zapped over and over. I have also seen people make short term "pens" so the animal is closely surrounded by the potential for electrocution.

- **Heartbreak 2:** Even when implemented properly, there is still that first zap. And it's a doozy. If you accidentally get zapped and you are screaming in pain, you might wonder how these animals survive such a shock. Overall, it feels a bit too much like a prison and not a soul-building experience.

- **Heartbreak 3:** All that plastic and the electrical challenges (big lead-acid batteries or getting grid power to the fence) seem contrary to my values.

Depending on where you live, you may have different fencing needs. At my place, we were trying to grow stuff, but the wild turkeys and the deer kept obliterating everything we were trying to grow. I wanted a fence that would allow us to keep chickens inside but would keep wild turkeys and deer outside. Looking at alternatives, field fence is fairly effective at all of the above, but it is very expensive and is generally painted or galvanized – toxins I would like to avoid. I'd like something a little more natural.

Hmmmm…good natural fences…I don't have bamboo (yet!). I don't have willow (yet!).[7] I have rocks,[8] but a deer fence has to be 8 feet (~2.5 meters) tall[9] – that's more rock than I have. Well…what do I have?[10]

I have so many conifer trees that if I don't get rid of a bunch, I am tempting a forest fire. Most people in my area with this problem will thin their forest under the name "reducing fuel load." They take all the trees they cut down and put them in a huge pile and burn the pile in the winter when it is safe. What a waste! Most of that wood is from thousands of young trees that died when they got to be about 12 feet (~4 meters) tall. A good deer fence is at least 8 feet (~2.5 meters) tall…

Here is design number 8 in using this material. I call it "junk pole fence."[11]

The junk pole tapers faster than bamboo, and it is not keen to weave like willow. We found we didn't need many nails to hold it together – most of the junk poles are loose. Maybe one in ten has a nail in it. The thick end at the bottom ends up making a pretty

7 permies.com/t/432 (willow fence)
8 permies.com/t/39351 (rock jacks)
9 permies.com/t/108915 (fence height)
10 permies.com/t/43425 (hedge plants)
11 permies.com/t/47946 (junk pole fence)

solid barrier – holding in the piglets, kids (aka baby goats), and the trickiest of all: chicks.

Field fence would cost about $150 per hundred feet. Junk pole fence costs less than $5 per hundred feet – 97% off! Once you have the materials gathered, it goes up pretty fast. It does still take longer to put up than a field fence, but for me the savings and the aesthetics are easily worth it.

If It Smells Bad, You're Doing It Wrong: Never Mucking out a Shelter Again

I think that an important aspect of caring for animals is providing them with a shelter that is warm, dry, and clean. Unfortunately, most animal shelters I have seen do not meet these criteria. More often than not, they are downright repulsive.

It seems that most people like to build stationary animal shelters. The big problem with stationary shelters is that all farm animals – except pigs, llamas, and alpacas – will poop and pee in their shelter. And they don't clean up after themselves. So it starts to accumulate. And stink.

The idea is that the human will come in regularly and clean out the shelter… except most humans find they don't like cleaning out a smelly shelter…so it happens less often than they intend. Some people will throw in a bunch of straw to soak up the smell, but that doesn't get rid of the poop. The dangers are still there. Again, I think we can do better for the animals.

I believe that nothing on a farm should smell. If it smells bad, you are doing it wrong.

I am a huge fan of portable shelters.[12] The draggable nature of a shelter built on skids is perfect for a paddock shift system. Simply hook up a truck, tractor, or large group of people (if that's your idea of fun) and move the shelter to the next paddock.

The key is to use a portable shelter with no floor. That way, when the shelter is moved, the poop stays where it is and the animals get fresh ground. When I move a skiddable shelter to a new area, I try to put it on the poorest soil. That spot will be the greenest, lushest part of the paddock next year. All without lifting a shovel.

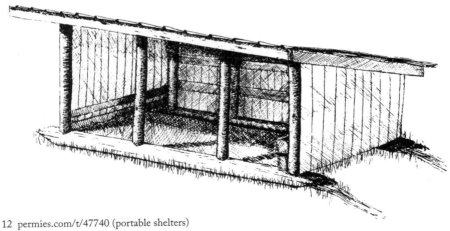

12 permies.com/t/47740 (portable shelters)

The Very Best Predator Control Is Not a Fence

When I moved onto my first farm, I was told that nobody in the neighborhood was able to raise chickens because there was such a serious coyote problem. Sure enough, I could hear them howling and yipping every night. But I was dead set on raising chickens. I told the neighbors that I would just build some super fence to keep the coyotes out, and they told me stories of people who built all sorts of amazing fences and still lost all of their chickens to coyotes. As if that isn't bad enough, weasels can get through or over nearly any fence you can dream of. And let's not forget about the predator air attack from eagles and hawks.

So I took to the internet. I found lots of people who had some wimpy fence and never had any predator trouble saying: "Do it like me! You won't have any problems! I promise!" I was tempted, but my gut said that these folks did not have the coyote challenge I faced and, if I tried to do what they did, all of my chickens would be killed.

Then I met a woman advocating dogs to protect the chickens. This struck me as not quite right because coyotes are rather dog-like, and I'd heard of people losing chickens to dogs. This woman had the patience to carefully explain to me that there are certain breeds of dogs that have been bred for thousands of years to protect livestock, including chickens.[13] These breeds of dogs are now very different from most breeds of dogs. These dogs would take on a mountain lion to try to save a chicken. The woman also told me about how she had built what she was sure was a coyote-proof fence only to lose every last chicken to coyotes. And then she got a Great Pyrenees dog, and she never lost a chicken to predators again.

After hearing from two more people with similar experiences with livestock guardian dogs, I bought a Great Pyrenees pup: Liza. Well, she wasn't a purebred. She had a little Anatolian Shepherd (another livestock guardian dog breed) and a pinch of Saint Bernard.

You could hear Liza battle the coyotes nearly every night. First, you'd hear the howling, and then about 3/4 of a second later, you'd hear Liza running by at full speed. About twelve seconds later, you'd hear the howling replaced by "Yipe! yipe! yipe!" She'd run them off.

She patrolled all night for predators. And if the chickens made a certain noise during the day, she was right there looking to see if there might be a threat.

That was 18 years ago. The path with a livestock guardian dog has been validated hundreds of times. If you have acreage, a livestock guardian breed of dog is the way to go. Everything becomes much easier and cheaper after that. And the animals will live more enjoyable lives without predators gobbling up their friends all the time.

13 permies.com/t/41833 (livestock guardian dogs)

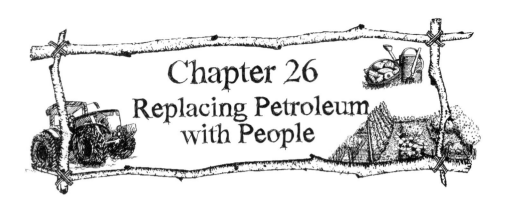

Chapter 26
Replacing Petroleum
with People

"What is in this chapter is basically what I am currently doing with a half million acres."

- Willie Smits[1]

Someone once asked me how I would do permaculture with 20,000 acres (~8000 hectares) of raw land (one acre is about the size of a football field). At the time, I had less than five minutes to convey my thoughts. Here is my answer, now with a bit of polish.

Let's start by looking at the conventional (or even "conventional" organic) path. 20,000 acres is 31.25 square miles (80.9 km²). A chunk of land of that size might include some mountains and some valleys. The conventional approach would be to run cattle on the mountains and then drain the swamps and convert the valleys to crop land.

Converting raw land to "productive" land takes time. Maybe a team of 30 or 40 people will clear the land, remove all of the stumps, drain the swamps, work the soil, and build up fences to make it suitable for conventional agriculture. It might take three years to get the first thousand acres from raw land into production. In ten years, all 20,000 acres are productive. Then it will be possible to drop down to 20 people.

Those people are going to need a place to stay, so there's an upfront investment in housing for 20-40 people. And then there's an upfront investment of roughly 10 million dollars on equipment and 10 million dollars on infrastructure such as machine sheds, grain bins, and irrigation systems. With such large start-up costs, it's going to take a while to break even – especially when you consider the need to cover the significant annual costs that come with conventional ag: seed, petroleum-based fuel, petroleum-based fertilizer, petroleum-based pesticides, energy for pumping water, etc.

Then it's time to play the commodity-farming game and mass-produce three to nine different products. If a few of those products have a rough year in the field or on the market, so do you. Plus, if you're hungry, you can't just walk into your field and grab a meal – you still need to go to a grocery store. And you have to spend most of your

1 permies.com/t/8596 (Willie Smits)

time with loud, smelly, petroleum-powered machinery.

Bill Mollison made it pretty clear that a big part of permaculture is replacing petroleum with people.[2]

If I had 20,000 acres, I would divide it into a hundred chunks – that's 200 acres (~80 hectares) per chunk. On each 200-acre chunk, I would select one person to be in charge, and then sprinkle in 12 to 30 people who would live there and work the permaculture system.

Rather than a monocrop focus, this would be a massively distributed, overlapping polyculture system. And rather than the 20,000 acres having one beekeeper managing 10,000 hives, there would be 500 beekeepers managing 3 to 30 hives each. Instead of one person doing only beekeeping, each person would manage 20 to 60 different crops or small enterprises.

Here again it's going to take some time to get the system going. For the first year, I would start off by selecting 10 of the 100 plots, then select leaders for those plots and begin constructing housing for 100 people. On top of that, some people would be focused on making five acres (two hectares) of each plot into a super awesome permaculture garden. It's not much (and not enough to sell), but it will provide some of the food for the people working on the land. And part of permaculture is "feed the people on the land first."

In three years there might be a total of 200 people on the land using the first 50 acres of each plot productively. After ten years, 2000 people and all 200 acres of each plot are productive, except maybe for the newest plots to be started – which are on their way.

The food produced from the 20,000 acres would first feed the roughly 2000 people who are now living there. And since 2000 people can manage the system much more intensively than a few people with big machines, there would still be a bunch of food left to sell.

For an apples-to-apples comparison, the whole system could still be set up for commodity farming. But rather than having three to nine products growing as 30 to 5000 acre (~10 to 2000 hectare) monocrops, the production would be distributed as part of a polyculture of over 100 products on 20,000 acres. Then one day, a semi truck would pull up and everyone would bring the extra tomatoes from their plot and load it up. On another day, they would load it up with chickens, and on yet another day, they would load it up with walnuts. If a few products don't do well in the field or on the market each year, it's not a problem – there are still 100 other products to carry the weight.[3]

This approach solves one of the biggest problems with small farming: marketing. Most farmers would rather spend their time farming instead of worrying about how they are actually going to sell their products. This is a big reason so many small farms fail to make money. On the other hand, a 20,000-acre, multi-million-dollar permaculture business could easily take the burden of marketing off the shoulders of the farmers.

As a bonus, while the potential to out-compete conventional ag in the commodity market exists here, there are opportunities that I think could bring in far more money:[4]

- marketing products directly to consumers
- value-added products

2 permies.com/t/59144 (Bill Mollison)
3 permies.com/t/87380 (business plans)
4 permies.com/t/2641 (income ideas)

- tourism/resort/glamping
- workshops
- weddings and events
- fine furniture, crafts, and other woodworking
- and many more…

Whether they just focus on farming or take on one of these extra ventures to boot, each person could receive a stable income while also having a beautiful place to live and delicious, healthy food to eat. Things might be so good that besides paying for their food and rent, they barely have any living expenses, allowing them to put aside a bunch of money in savings each year. Maybe someday they'll go buy their own acreage…but things are pretty good where they are.

By relying on people to do most of the work with hand tools, we would drastically reduce the petroleum footprint of our operation.[5] That said, there would be a few times when petroleum might still be used to accomplish a task, such as using an excavator to build ponds. Once built, the ponds would require no petroleum inputs to maintain. And, spreading the amount of petroleum used in construction over the lifetime of the pond, the fuel use would be practically negligible. Especially when compared to the annual inputs of chem ag.

The start-up cost of the permaculture system is mostly in housing and the people to implement the system, while equipment and infrastructure costs are a tiny fraction of a conventional system. And we've eliminated the need to buy fuel, fertilizer, and pesticides year after year. Rather than pouring money into petroleum, we're investing money in people.

5 permies.com/t/65641 (people vs petroleum)

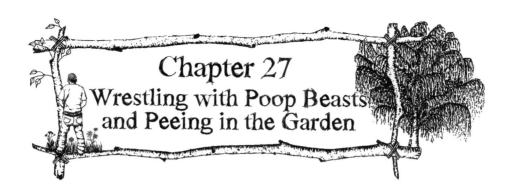

Chapter 27
Wrestling with Poop Beasts and Peeing in the Garden

In chapter 22, we talked about the different levels of wastewater management one might achieve. And we talked about some ways of treating greywater – almost all of which are theoretically possible with an urban lot. But we intentionally left the discussion of what to do with blackwater until here in Part 5 because it's generally easier to deal with appropriately when you live on a homestead.

Most of us have been taught that pee and poop are waste and must be removed from the premises with the utmost expediency, lest we all die of an unfortunate illness. While there is good reason for caution, something else to consider is that our urine and feces are loaded with all of the extra nutrients from our food that our bodies did not use – nutrients that could eventually help grow more food. To send those nutrients "away" is a waste. In other words, it is a waste to call this material a waste. I want to keep these nutrients on my land – but I want to do so safely.

Creating a Magnificent Jungle with Your Urine

Even if you have some kind of crazy infection, fresh urine is still sterile for all practical purposes.[1] In rare cases, urine can contain pathogens – but then those pathogens will survive no more than seven seconds outside the human body. Medical professionals do not require the use of gloves when dealing with human urine.

There are some people who, for their own reasons, drink urine. Just like with brussels sprouts, I am constantly baffled by what people choose to put in their pie holes. But I think this makes a good point that brussels sprouts, despite their horrible flavor, are considered safe to consume. And urine falls into that same category.

Urine contains a very particular mix of nitrogen, phosphorus, and potassium (N,P,K) that happens to be a really good fertilizer.[2] And using our urine to feed some growies is a great way of recycling our nutrients back into our gardening systems. It's as if people are meant to be gardeners!

Some people will capture their urine in some sort of container, dilute it with water, and then use it to irrigate the base of their plants. Urine has a lot of nitrogen, so diluting it helps to prevent "burning" the plants.[3] Urine can also contain a fair bit of

1 permies.com/t/722 (urine sterility)
2 permies.com/t/4876 (urine fertilizer)
3 permies.com/t/85068 (burning plants)

salt, so dilution helps keep the concentration at a manageable level for soil organisms.[4]

Another approach is to pee at the base of the plants instead of fussing with a container filled with pee water. If it has been raining or is about to rain, I will pee near plants that love a lot of nitrogen like rhubarb, grasses, cottonwood, willow, or poplar.[5] And if it is currently raining, I might just pee near any plant – the rain will take care of dilution. But if it hasn't rained for a couple of days and won't rain for a couple more days, then the urine needs to be diluted or even the most nitrogen-loving plants might get sad.

The trick is to pee in one spot – let the plants take what they want. If you pee everywhere around a plant, then it is left with no choice. Another way of thinking of it: add diversity to the soil rather than making the soil homogeneous. Some spots have more pee than other spots – so plants that like lots of pee can have more of it. And plants that don't like pee so much can opt out.

Peeing on good soil works about a hundred times better than peeing on dirt. Pee and dirt makes for stinky mud. Most plants are just not into that sort of kink. Rich soil is loaded with carbon and micro-organisms – this team of about 400 trillion beasties has been craving some good urine, and their new slogan is "WE'RE RICH! WE'RE RICH! IN ALL OF OUR DEEPEST FANTASIES, WE NEVER IMAGINED SUCH AMAZING WEALTH!" This is the part where you can tell this massive population "Yes, I am a generous god."

At this point, I expect that a number of you reading this will say "BUT Paul, I'm a woman! We can't just pee outside!" In response, I will say that I know plenty of women who choose to pee outdoors on a regular basis. I hear that for some women it just takes a bit of practice and ingenuity. And for others it takes a bit of practice, ingenuity, and determination.[6]

To be fair, regardless of what body parts you might have, peeing outdoors can lead to some uncomfortable conversations with neighbors and, potentially, officers of the law. If you live near other people, you may wish to stick with the urine diverter and container approach. Just don't tell the neighbors what's in the watering can…

Before moving on, I want to quickly include a few words of caution. While urine is usually just fine when fresh, it starts to get pretty rich with bacteria if you let it sit. After roughly 24 hours, urine will start turning into ammonia and develop a powerful stink! After being stored long enough, the ammonia kills off any bacteria…but you also lose a lot of the nitrogen (which is the smell – the nitrogen escaping into the atmosphere). It's best applied fresh.

An Exploration of Pooping Contraptions

In chapter 20, we explored the idea of NOT composting.[7] The same can be said for composting toilets – that's a lot of carbon and nitrogen that we want to keep in our soils rather than sending it up into the atmosphere. But, poop from sick people can contain dangerous pathogens that can make other people sick. So we need to remove the pathogens while keeping the carbon and nitrogen.

To explore "better" or "best," we need to parade out the options and metrics.

---

4 permies.com/t/22926 (removing salt from urine)
5 ermies.com/t/32638 (urine-loving plants)
6 permies.com/t/3965 (women peeing outdoors)
7 permies.com/t/43333 (not composting)

The nominees for the best place to put your poop are (in no particular order):

- **Poop on the ground:** in tropical areas, the poop will generally be gone in a few hours – but it can still make people sick. In colder climates, the danger lasts much longer.

- **Poop in a hole:** dig a hole, poop in it, and cover up the hole. The worst part of backpacking.

- **Outhouse:** a big hole in the ground with a little structure built over it.

- **Septic tank & drain field:** a standard flush toilet connected to a septic tank and drain field in your yard.

- **Sewage treatment plant:**[8] a standard flush toilet connected to a municipal sewer system.

- **Humanure:**[9] fill a five-gallon (~20 liter) bucket with poop, pee, and sawdust and twice a week put it in a compost pile outside.

- **Composting toilet:**[10] the poop goes into a chamber. Fresh material is added on top and finished material is pulled out the bottom. The contraption might have something that attempts to speed up the composting process.

- **Poop cooker:** a composting toilet with an electric heating element inside of it that heats the poop for ten minutes to sterilize it.

- **Willow feeder:**[11] poop is stored for two years to eliminate pathogens and then placed at the base of willow trees. More on this later.

- **Dry outhouse:**[12] like an outhouse except with a urine diverter and placed on a hill where rain doesn't reach the pit. Nutrient-loving trees are planted around the structure to drink up the nutrients. More on this later.

There are several more options to add to this list, but this is enough to make my points.

For each system, there are several possible metrics. Of course, there's a lot of "it depends" involved, but I am going to make up a number for each metric for each system to try to paint a picture of how each performs relative to the others without going too much into the nitty gritty. Each factor will be ranked from 0 to 10, with "0" representing "worst" and "10" representing "best."

The six metrics under consideration are:

- **The stink factor:** can we just make a system that doesn't stink? Something that people like to use more than the modern bathroom?

- **The fly factor:** a fly lands on poop and then lands on your food and you get sick.

- **The poop-flavored water factor:** poop finds its way into the groundwater and you get sick.

- **The poop handling factor:** how much gross poop handling is involved in the operation?

8 permies.com/t/18791 (sewer treatment podcast)
9 permies.com/t/44341 (humanure)
10 permies.com/t/571 (composting toilets)
11 permies.com/t/25481 (willow feeders)
12 permies.com/t/953 (dry outhouses)

- **The fertilizer factor:** how much of the nutrients are repurposed as fertilizer?
- **The price factor:** it would be nice to have a good solution that doesn't break the bank.

And now for the comparison (remember, "10" is best):

	Stink factor	Fly factor	Poop-flavored water factor	Poop handling factor	Fertilizer factor	Price factor
Poop on the ground	2	0	1	4	7	10
Poop in a hole	5	5	1	4	8	9
Outhouse	1	0	1	8	1	7
Septic tank & drain field	6	10	4	8	0	1
Sewage treatment plant	6	8	6	8	0	0
Humanure	3	4	2	0	4	4-8
Composting toilet	5	10	6	6	4	4
Poop cooker	6	10	10	7	10	6
Willow feeder	9-10	10	10	8	8	4-6
Dry outhouse	10	10	9.5	10	10	7

Of these options, I think the willow feeder and the dry outhouse are the best bet. Let's take a closer look at each of them.

Making Poop Jerky and Saving It for Later

On my property I have several willow feeders.[13] Mine are all in skiddable structures, but this design could also be used for an indoor toilet. The design is that there is a big, watertight garbage can that receives the deposit in a chamber underneath the seat. The idea is that the garbage can is really close to the hole so there is no chance of anything ending up outside the can...no matter how much digestive distress the supplier might have!

When poop and pee are mixed together, it makes things stinkier. And when pee is included, there is a lot of extra moisture that often needs to be taken up, usually with sawdust. A big part of my design is that a urine diverter is included to catch 90% of the pee (that wasn't already deposited elsewhere) and send it outside. The bins fill up much less quickly and are much less smelly.

At the same time, air needs to be able to move from the sitting room, through the seat, into the garbage can chamber, and then up a vent pipe, which pulls excess stink and moisture out of the system. The vent is attached to a fly trap so that any flies that somehow make it down the hole and get covered in poop bits can't get out and transfer those poop bits onto people.

13 permies.com/t/47814 (another willow feeder)

In my experiments, I have employed both a solar-electric fan and a trombe wall to vent the space. The solar-electric fan generally works, but it involves using a battery which will need replacing roughly every five years and involves moving parts – not ideal. On the other hand, a trombe wall does not require active components. Sunlight passes through glass and strikes a thermal mass made of cob (a mix of clay, sand, and sometimes straw) with the vent pipe embedded in it. An air gap between the cob and the glass helps to hold the heat in. And since the pipe will be warmer inside the thermal mass than in the poop chamber, the air is drawn up the vent pipe by convection. This technique has been successful, even in the cold of a Montana winter!

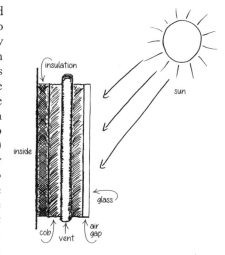

Once the bins are full, they are sealed off so that no one opens them and they are allowed to sit for two whole years. After this point 99.999% of the pathogens in the bin will be dead – if there ever were any pathogens. To be clear, this is NOT designed to be a composting toilet that composts all of the materials – I'm trying for "poop mummification" or "making poop jerky" where most of the carbon and nitrogen is still in the bin at the end. But so far we have found that a can appears half full after sitting for two years, so the material has broken down a little anyways. Still, when the bin is opened after two years, you will see poop jerky and the accompanying toilet paper… but the pathogens are dead so it's now safe to use.

Some people would feel just fine with placing the finished material in their garden around all of their food crops. After all, the idea is to cycle the nutrients back into the food. I prefer to play it *extra* safe by placing the contents of the can at the base of willow, cottonwood, or poplar trees (that is, away from edible plants) and covering them up with sawdust. I refer to these tree species as "poop beasts" – plants that thrive in nutrient-rich environments.[14] They will happily eat up all of the nutrients provided by the finished material, bringing them back into the ecological system. Maybe someday they'll get cut down and put in a hugelkultur bed.[15] And then the nutrients will have come full circle.

Feeding Poop Beasts, Killing Them, and Building Stuff out of Their Bones

I think that the best solution is the dry outhouse. Let's take a regular outhouse and pimp it out so that we might score a 10 in the first five poop management metrics:

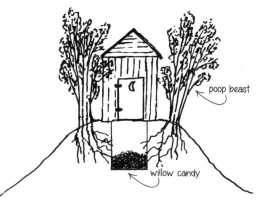

14 permies.com/t/1281 (poop beasts)
15 permies.com/t/hugelkultur

1. Include a urine diverter.

2. Use a vent system like the one for the willow feeder. (Remember, this also keeps the stink and flies under control.)

3. Place the dry outhouse on top of a ground swell that effectively sheds water and doesn't allow rain or ground water to reach the pit.

4. Plant poop beasts around the structure such that their roots will make their way into the pit and eat up all of the nutrients. The roots will also drink up any excess moisture.

How do those metrics look now?

- **The stink factor:** the regular outhouse might be one of the most horrible experiences a person could have. But the dry outhouse will keep air moving from the "people chamber" through "the hole" and up above the roof – so there will be less odor than a conventional bathroom.

- **The fly factor:** a regular outhouse could host fly conventions. A dry outhouse has no more flies than any other outdoor structure.

- **The poop-flavored water factor:** this is the main reason that the regular outhouse was made illegal. And while there could possibly be a tiny speck of liquid that might someday find its way to the groundwater, the odds are very near zero. And if any does, it would still be less than a septic tank or a sewage treatment plant.

- **The poop handling factor:** Some old-school outhouses were emptied. But the dry outhouse would never be emptied.

- **The fertilizer factor:** Regular outhouses did not typically feed plants, but the primary function of the dry outhouse is to feed the poop beasts.

With so little moisture, it might be possible that the hole will never fill up – the poop beasts will just gobble up everything that gets put in there. If it does, or if there is any other reason, it's a skiddable structure – you can just move the structure to a new location and drop a few seeds in the old hole. No poop handling required!

Of course, in some locations, the roots of the poop beasts will go dormant for winter. Fortunately, during this time the poop will freeze, and since there's so little moisture, the chances of groundwater contamination are very low. Then when the poop beasts wake up in the spring, they have a lot of poop-beast food ready to help them put on a lot of growth.

The only downside is that the seat might be a bit chilly in winter. But if you have an outdoor dry outhouse, you also have a great place to dump the contents from your indoor willow feeder! The best of all worlds!

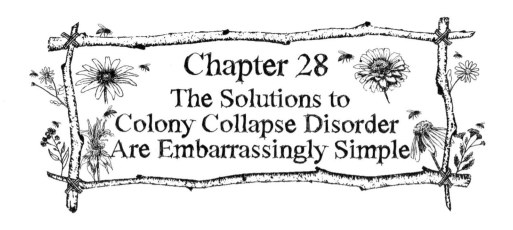

Chapter 28
The Solutions to
Colony Collapse Disorder
Are Embarrassingly Simple

"Though the problems of the world are increasingly complex, the solutions remain embarrassingly simple."

- Bill Mollison[1]

In 2006, beekeepers began reporting that their bees were disappearing en masse. The bees appeared to just leave the hive and never come back. The reports kept coming in and the losses being reported were as high as 40%! Later reports were as high as 80%! Of course, the first question that gets asked in such a situation is "What's causing it?"

Some research suggests that it is a virus or a fungus, or a combination of both. Other research suggests it is increased pest pressure, and other research suggests that it is neonicotinoid insecticides being used on crops. Here's the thing: I don't think it's just one thing, or even three things, that are causing the problem. I think that if the bees have poor nutrition, get covered in poison in the field, have poison in their home, and face all sorts of other stresses, each of these is going to weaken them. At some point all of the stresses are just too much.[2]

My friend, Jacqueline Freeman, wrote an excellent book called *Song of Increase: Listening to the Wisdom of Honeybees for Kinder Beekeeping and a Better World*.[3] In her book, she tells the story of watching a bee returning from foraging and being barred from entering by the colony's guard bees. After so many foraging flights, the bee's

wings were tattered. After two refusals by the guards, the old bee acknowledged the assessment of the guard bees and did a voluntary "walk the plank" maneuver, falling from the hive and ending up, plop, on the ground. Aside from the tattered wings, the bee looked okay to Jacqueline. She thought the guards must have made a mistake, so she picked up the bee and put it back at the hive entrance. But the bee was committed to leaving the hive and walked right off the edge, never to return.

1 permies.com/t/59144 (Bill Mollison)
2 permies.com/t/5155 (colony collapse disorder)
3 permies.com/t/44830 (*Song of Increase*)

Jacqueline believes the old bee embraced that, **maybe, the greatest contribution to the colony would be a voluntary departure.** Honey bees cannot survive without a colony, so the old bee was likely dead by morning.

Jacqueline also believes that, although most bees live only six weeks, a colony of bees maintains a memory that goes back decades. Maybe more. You might want to read her book to better understand how that might be possible, but for now, my next point embraces this idea.

The goal of each colony is to thrive, grow, and then swarm to create new colonies. Because of their generational memory, a colony might know that they are not thriving as previous colonies have. Therefore, something must be wrong with this colony. And, **maybe, the greatest contribution to future colonies would be a voluntary departure.** I suspect that it is not calculated or reasoned so much as there is some sort of instinctual metric that measures growth, and some sort of "fail" alarm goes off when the conditions are bad enough.

Jacqueline's book is called *The Song of Increase* because the colony makes a different

 sound for each general colony-wide activity. The best sound is the sound made during strong, vibrant, healthy growth: "the song of increase." I suggest that there is a different sound that signals "disperse." Maybe some of the bees join other colonies, but most, including the queen, simply go off alone and die quickly. This is my theory on why the colony collapse disorder hives are not full of dead bees, but are simply empty.

With that in mind, I think that the entire solution to colony collapse disorder can be summed up in four words: Stop stressing the bees.

While conventional beekeepers lose 40% of their colonies annually, organic beekeepers report 10% losses. And beekeepers who follow treatment-free methods using feral bees tend to have near-zero losses. The more in line with nature the practices are, the lower the losses are.[4]

My suggestions for healthy bee colonies:

1. When a colony is struggling, the conventional beekeeper looks to "attack and kill" the problem. Most "problems" are an aspect of nature working as it is supposed to. Focus on long-term, natural bee health instead of "attack and kill."

2. Bees get mites. Conventional beekeepers use poison in the hives in the hopes of killing more mites than bees. Many "treatment-free" beekeepers have proven techniques that show that the stress of a few mites is far less than the stress of these poisons.

3. Do not buy conventional packaged bees. These bees are bred for scale and not for strong genetics. And they are often dependent on chemical defenses instead of natural defenses. Catching a local, feral bee swarm will bring you bees that are naturally strong for your local conditions.[5]

4. Conventional beekeepers force a larval cell size that leads to larger/smaller

4 permies.com/t/1550 (beyond organic bees)
5 permies.com/t/24749 (catching swarms)

bees (thus, contrary to their natural size) by using premade plastic foundation. Allow bees to pick their own cell size.[6]

5. Weak colonies dependent on medications or unable to defend themselves against predators must be allowed to die out – thus improving the gene pool.

6. Migratory beekeepers chase bloom and move their hives thousands of miles every year. Keep hives in a fixed location year round.

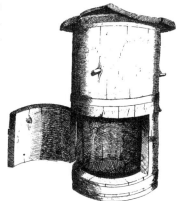

7. Conventional beekeepers take nearly all the honey and feed sugar water to the bees. Bees are designed to eat their own nutritious honey, not sugar water. Take less and allow the bees to eat their own honey.

8. Plant lots of three-season nectar forage so the bees don't have to travel more than a few hundred feet (~100 meters) for food (rather than several miles for more conventional approaches).[7]

9. Keep hives a hundred yards (~100 meters) or more apart. In nature, colonies live great distances apart. This reduces the need to compete for nearby food and prevents bees from drifting into other colonies and spreading pests and diseases.

10. Strong, healthy plants grown in a polyculture have richer, higher-quality nectar. Feed bees polyculture blossoms.

11. Stop using insecticides on crops – bees are insects!

12. Raising hives off the ground like natural hives reduces moisture problems in the hive. The higher the better.

13. Sheltered hives (sometimes called "bee huts") reduce bee stress and help keep the hive warmer in winter.[8]

14. Colonies that live in hollow tree trunks with 3-4 inch (~7-10 centimeter) thick walls are stronger because they can better control their own temperature and moisture. Build thick-walled hives instead of scrawny, conventional hive boxes.[9]

15. Mold is like the kiss of death for bees. If something is moldy, throw it away and replace it.

16. Conventional beekeepers open their hives for inspection weekly or bi-weekly. Bees in a proper home do best when they control their own environment with little or zero intervention.[10]

17. Use organic (or better) practices in everything you do, because it all comes back to the bees.

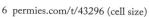

6 permies.com/t/43296 (cell size)
7 permies.com/t/15107 (nectar forage)
8 permies.com/t/37135 (bee hut)
9 permies.com/t/32735 (Holzer bee hive)
10 permies.com/t/61884 (hands-off bees)

By following these techniques, there could be 10% losses for the first three years as genetics get sorted out, and then there will be near-zero colony loss.

Four other chapters about animal care (chickens,[11] cattle,[12] hogs,[13] and aquaculture[14]) were eliminated in favor of keeping this one, because this chapter paints a really good picture of the general permaculture approach to working with nature instead of against nature. This chapter is meant to be an example of animal care far better than what is commonly practiced in producing a large part of our food. This book is not about animal care, but about building a better world. And this part is about helping people understand a flavor of animal care that not only makes for healthier, happier animals, but a healthier, happier everything! Nurture nature and nature nurtures us all.

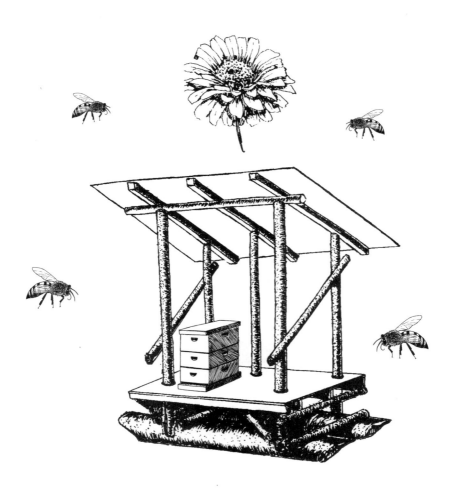

11 richsoil.com/chickens (raising chickens)
12 permies.com/t/22105 (winter cattle grazing)
13 permies.com/t/3367 (raising pigs)
14 permies.com/t/2512 (pond farming)

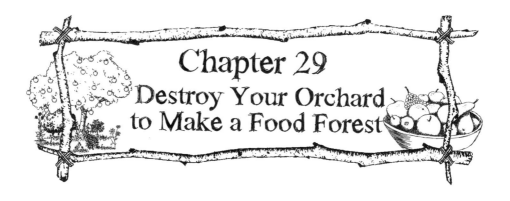

Chapter 29
Destroy Your Orchard to Make a Food Forest

The most frustrating question I hear is "How do I turn my orchard into a permaculture orchard?" I tell people to start by cutting down 90% of their trees. Their counterpoint tends to feature harsh words and sometimes pitchforks and other stabby tools.

I think that when most people hear the word "orchard," they think of a classic orchard with 15-foot-high (~5 meter) trees surrounded by neatly mowed grass.

But modern orchards look much different. The trees are planted on dwarf rootstock so that they are incapable of growing much more than 8 feet (~3 meters) tall. And the trees are trained into shapes that are so unnatural, they need wires to help hold up their branches.

I think that the term "permaculture orchard" is an oxymoron.[1] An apple orchard, for example, is several rows of apple trees. A perennial monocrop. As with most monocrops, the plants (trees) all need the same things from the soil, and they all put the same exudates into the soil. If one plant gets hit with some sort of pest, it quickly spreads to all the others. Suddenly the insecticides and fungicides are looking mighty tempting.

But if we limit the number of trees of each species to no more than 10%, then the apple tree is surrounded by trees that are not apple trees. And instead of just trees

1 permies.com/t/36584 (permaculture orchard podcast)

surrounded by grass, we can include useful species from all seven layers of a forest: overstory, understory, shrubs, herbs, ground covers, root crops, and vines.[2]

Food forest layers
1 overstory
2 understory
3 shrub layer
4 herbaceous layer
5 ground cover layer
6 root layer
7 vine layer
▨ shade lovers

In a couple of years, this food forest will be so lush that the sun will rarely reach the soil.

The root exudate of these other species is food for the apple tree and the root exudate of the apple tree is food for the other species.[3] Perhaps some of the neighboring trees are nitrogen-fixing species and are generous with their nitrogen. And perhaps another nearby plant creates a compound that repels certain pests and diseases, sharing it with other plants through the exchanges between roots and mycelium. The impact of pests and diseases is dramatically reduced.

If, despite our abundant polyculture, a particular tree gets taken out by pest or disease, then that means that nature did not want that tree there. It's probably not worth the effort in trying to save it – we are better off working with nature than against nature.[4]

As mentioned earlier, I believe an important aspect of working with nature is to plant all of your growies from seed instead of transplanting. For starters, this approach avoids digging a hole for each tree and saves a lot of money on buying pre-grown trees. The main reason that I avoid transplanting is that, when you transplant your growies, they lose their tap root[5] – a singular thick root that many plants have that anchors them in the ground and can reach water and nutrients that are too deep for shallow-rooted plants. It turns out that plants don't like being moved and can take months or years to recover. Oftentimes, a tree planted from seed will catch up with a transplanted tree within three to five years.

By planting trees from seed, we are playing the lottery with plant varieties.[6] We will find a few new cultivars that are terrible. We can cut those down and use that wood

2 permies.com/t/61334 (starting a food forest)
3 permies.com/t/83769 (exudates)
4 permies.com/t/20694 (working with nature)
5 permies.com/t/998 (seeding vs transplanting)
6 permies.com/t/31939 (plant varieties)

for a variety of other things. We will also find some new cultivars that are excellent. These new cultivars will work best with the conditions on our land, not some place far away with totally different conditions. This will make the trees more disease resistant, more insect resistant, healthier, and more productive than if we just bought some trees from the store and stuck them in the ground.

Pruning trees trains them to require further pruning. In an orchard, the trees are pruned at least once, if not multiple times, per year to get that perfect figure. It's a lot of work. Masanobu Fukuoka[7] tried to stop pruning his trees. The trees died. Then he planted new trees and pretty much never pruned them.[8] The trees grew much bigger and were much healthier. They had a conelike shape with big branches right next to the ground, which left much less chance for things to grow under the tree and compete for nutrients.

The fruit of the "cone tree" is divided into three portions. The bottom portion is left to the critters and turned into eggs and meat (chicken, pork, duck, etc.); the middle portion is harvested for fresh eating, drying, juicing, and canning; and the top portion is left for the birds so they eat less of the stuff within easy reach of human harvesters. Some of that top fruit will eventually fall and become winter feed for your animals.[9]

Fruit left on the ground becomes a vector for pests and diseases. Animals eating that fruit eliminates that problem. Bacon-flavored pest control!

Rather than a harvest of one kind of fruit in an orchard, we can now harvest a hundred different products throughout a growing season with less work.

7 permies.com/t/2214 (Masanobu Fukuoka)
8 permies.com/t/2590 (not pruning)
9 permies.com/t/1315 (winter feed)

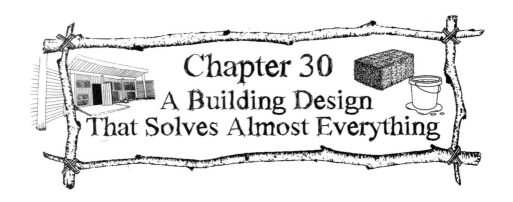

Chapter 30
A Building Design
That Solves Almost Everything

This chapter is not for the faint of heart. This is what I recommend for what I believe to be the ultimate permaculture scenario. I imagine that no one below eco level 4 would ever consider actually doing this, and yet I think some people below eco level 4 will read this chapter anyways just to come along for the ride.

If you're looking at a building design, you're likely going to be looking for land on which to build it. So before we move on to building design, I wish to take this opportunity to state that, in my opinion, a sloped woodland in a colder climate is far superior to all other options. Soil generally builds fastest in a cold climate. And if you live some place where it's flat, you can't control the movement of frost and water on your land. And if you live where there's too little rainfall, you can make it work, but it's going to be far slower – and you won't already have trees to work with. As a bit of bonus luck, the flat land I don't want tends to appeal to conventional farmers – which means the ultimate permaculture land seems like the cheapest land around!

There are many different schools of thought in the world of "sustainable" building. Unfortunately in most cases the environmental footprint is still really big, even for platinum LEED.[1] That said, there have been some designs that have come out that are pretty good. But although there are people who would argue otherwise, I am going to suggest that no single design is suitable for every location. And it turns out that for sloped woodland in a colder climate, these designs all fall short for some reason or another.

After years of researching natural building techniques, I came up with a design for sloped woodland that creates a beautiful living space with an extremely low footprint. Imagine living in something that, from the inside, looks like a log cabin with more light; doesn't need heat or A/C; is three times faster to build; and has about one-fifth of the materials cost. I call it "wofati."[2] And I believe this building design is so good that some people might just move to a sloped woodland in order to embrace it.

The intricate details of this design can easily fill a book. We are currently wrapping up some builds[3] and some experiments,[4] and it is now safe to share a few of the details here!

1 permies.com/t/leed
2 permies.com/t/wofati
3 permies.com/t/26205 (wofati 0.7)
4 permies.com/t/33160 (wofati 0.8)

Setting Our Design Criteria Extremely High

The following are the main criteria I looked for in a natural building design:

- More than half of the materials come from the property
- One-hundredth the toxicity of a conventional home
- A structure that will last at least 50 years
- Heating efficiency better than passive solar
- Easy for a first-time builder to build
- Materials + labor = less than a conventional home
- A beautiful, luxuriant space to live in

Before we get into the wofati, let's take a look at some other popular building styles and see how they match up against some of these criteria.

We Can Do Better Than Straw Bale Designs

A straw bale home is often essentially the same as a conventional home except the exterior walls are replaced by straw bales covered in plaster. Some builders report that it is a bit like building the exterior walls twice: once with wood, to hold up the roof, and a second time to add the straw bales.[5]

The beauty of straw bale is the insulation. Straw itself is not a particularly good insulator, but a really thick wall of it is, so straw bale homes usually end up much more insulated than conventional homes. This reduces the need to heat the home during the winter. Of course, to stay warm on a really cold day it helps if you're sealed up inside like being in a ziplock bag.

When paying for the labor, straw bale homes are typically 30% more expensive than conventional homes. Some people host a workshop on their build site to mitigate this expense.

The upside is that you're sequestering carbon. The downside is that this building style relies somewhat heavily on the existence of annual grain monocrops…something I would like to move away from. And unless you live on land that produces straw, you will have to buy straw and have it moved to you. For people who live in the mountains, that's a long distance for the straw to travel.[6] I wish for something more local.

We Can Do Better Than Cob Designs

As with straw bale, cob construction generally still has a conventional roof and foundation. Instead of straw covered in plaster, the walls are made of sand, clay, and a bit of some sort of fiber (often chopped straw).[7]

5 permies.com/f/73 (straw bale forum)
6 permies.com/t/18358 (shipping bales)
7 permies.com/f/76 (cob forum)

The material costs for a cob wall will be lower than for a conventional wall. That said, as much fun as it is to think about building a home just from the dirt in your yard, for quality cob you need a source of clay and good sand. Not just any sand will do. Sometimes you are on land that has clay, so then you just need a few dump truck loads of sand. If you're really lucky you'll have both.

The beauty of cob is that you can shape it to anything. And it is soooooo easy to do. Cob homes can be extremely beautiful.[8] But! The amount of time needed to build a cob wall is far greater than a conventional wall. If you can supply lots of time, you can build a fantastically lovely home from cob for a reasonable price. On the other hand, if you're paying someone to build it for you, it's going to cost you big time. I wish for something that's just as easy to build as cob, but faster.

This is a good time to point out that there are cob structures which have a more-natural-than-most roof and foundation. A "good hat and good boots" can be timber with EPDM (pond liner) for the roof, and rocks and cob for the floor. The structures by Ianto Evans at Cob Cottage are a great example.[9]

The Dirty Secret of "Sustainable" Building

It seems to me that a lot of "sustainable" or "natural" homes use a lot of cement. Sometimes there's a huge slab for the foundation, sometimes there's a basement, and sometimes it's even a part of the walls (such as with cordwood or stone buildings).

In my travels, I haven't noticed wild cement lying around, just waiting for that special person to come along and whip it up into a new slab floor.

To make cement, you need to heat calcium to a very high temperature for a long time. If you were going to build a cement pad for a home, and you were going to make your own cement, you might need a hundred cords of wood.[10] That is a big slice of forest. And that is a lot of carbon in the atmosphere. Plus, it would probably take you more than a year to convert that calcium and pull together all of the ingredients for the cement. As for the calcium, where did you get that? Do you happen to have a small mountain of seashells at your place?

Lastly, it is my feeling (you have license to have different feelings) that cement tends to take a bit of soul out of a home, whereas a material like cob tends to **add** a bit of soul to a home.

The Joy and Heartbreak of Earthships

When I was a pup, my Earthship book was in tatters from too much love. When Christmas rolled around, everybody's gift from me was a brand new Earthship book. By the time I got land where I could build my first Earthship, my values had become richer, and I had learned a lot more about Earthships that had dimmed my enthusiasm.[11]

For those that don't know, an Earthship is a south-facing building where the walls are

8 permies.com/t/43488 (beautiful cob)
9 permies.com/t/49633 (Ianto Evans)
10 permies.com/t/16304 (homemade cement)
11 permies.com/t/1140 (Earthships)

built with old tires. Well, there is a lot more to it. They are beautiful. And...did I mention the old tires?

When you hold the book in your hand, your brain is locked on how simple and brilliant this technique is. And using stuff from the waste stream instead of filling dumps with toxic gick sounds great! It probably took me about ten years of stars in my eyes until somebody pointed out "So you want to live with the toxic gick in your house?"[12] This is where the heartbreak started. Ouch.

I wish to thank Michael Reynolds for bringing the Earthship into reality and giving us all this magnificent dream and world-changing stepping-stone. I have elected to try to keep all of the best parts of the Earthship design in the wofati design while mitigating the downsides. Since the new design is so far removed from being an Earthship, and since there are so many downsides of an Earthship, the new design needed a whole new name. I guess this is a long-winded way of saying that I hope Michael Reynolds will forgive me for moving on to the wofati design.

Prevent Wildfires by Building a Home

As mentioned in chapter 25, if you don't thin your forest properly, you could lose all of your trees (and possibly your vehicle, home, life, etc.) to wildfires. Most of the time, when the forest needs thinning, the price that the mill will pay for wood is less than what you might pay to get the wood to the mill. As a result, a lot of folks who need to thin their trees end up burning this wood for no productive purpose and release the carbon into the atmosphere. Such a waste! I want to sequester that carbon and use it to build a house!

We are now talking about good forestry management. But I would like to go three steps further to what I call "good woodland management." Rather than using forestry practices that are for one person managing 1000 acres (~400 hectares) of forest, I prefer techniques for one person developing a symbiotic relationship with 20 acres (~8 hectares) of woodland. That person lives on the 20 acres, is bonkers about permaculture, and is transforming the land from a conifer forest to what more closely resembles a huge garden loaded with a diversity of trees. Maybe 10% of the land will be "conifer islands" but the rest of the land will be broadleaf trees. This means that 90% or more of the conifers on the land need to go. And into a home on that very land is the best possible use.

To be clear, I am not advocating building a log cabin. It is very hard to stay warm in a log cabin in the winter – the insulation value is low and there is very little thermal mass. Plus, log cabins require a lot of very specifically sized, fairly large trees – not a great fit for forest thinnings. The wofati design uses just a few big logs for the frame and then thinnings for the rest, so my design prevents forest fires, and I get free building materials at the same time!

From Junk to Genius with One Simple Design Change

80% of my design stands on the rather brilliant shoulders of the late Mike Oehler.[13] In the fall of 1970, Mike lived in a crappy shack and struggled to stay warm. He decided that the following spring he would build a better place to live. He spent the winter drawing all sorts of designs to calculate heat efficiency. He also wanted to keep his

---

12 permies.com/t/74736 (tire toxicity)
13 permies.com/t/43114 (Mike Oehler)

material costs low. He came up with a design that was unlike anything he had ever seen anywhere else.

Mike's design eliminates many of the complexities of conventional construction. Further, if you live on wooded land, most of the required materials consist of what you cut from your land when doing sustainable forestry thinning. No importing straw bales or dump truck loads of sand. In fact, everything you import could fit into one pickup load: some doors, some glass, some plumbing and electrical stuff – all of which you would bring in for any type of house.

In a nutshell, Mike's design is a pole structure with a green roof. This usually means a structure surrounded by a waterproof membrane and then covered with dirt. A green roof is usually more expensive than a conventional roof, but Mike found that if you can follow one simple design principle, you can dramatically cut the costs of the whole structure!

The one simple design principle is this:

Every drop of rain must have a complete downhill soil path and must never encounter the edge of a roof.

In order to illustrate this principle, we're going to try to show the water flow for various designs. The shading will be darker where there is more water in the soil. With a conventional home, if you put in a little wrap-around ditch on the uphill side, water is managed like so:

In his book, Mike Oehler describes a "first-thought house" – the first design people generally think of when they think of a house with a green roof. I call it a "don't-do-this house."

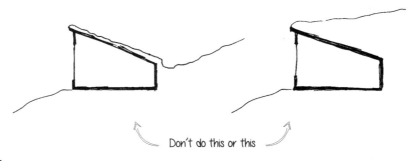

Don't do this or this

People tend to think of the second design more than the first. But where does all of the extra dirt come from? Are you also digging a big hole somewhere nearby? Let's drop that design and focus on the first one. This might be a good time to include a reminder that the wofati design is intended for sloped land. Otherwise there is a lot of dirt that needs moving!

Here's what happens when it rains:

This is where all of the people with this terrible design start doing their pseudo engineering. The first thought is to put a French drain on the uphill side. But a French drain is designed to deal with the water table getting too high – not with too much water coming from above.[14] So while that might help a little, it really doesn't work. A wraparound ditch around the back might help a little, but most of the water is already below the soil level and yet still above floor level inside the house.

The bottom line is that people who use this design end up with something that smells like a musty basement and is so riddled with water problems that thousands of these homes are abandoned. I could go on about this, but Mike's book does a much better job of bashing this design.[15]

Let's fix the primary problem with the "don't-do-this house" design:

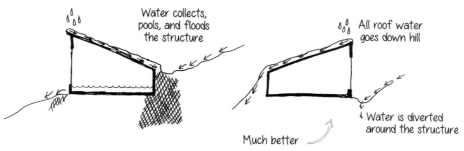

Water collects, pools, and floods the structure

Much better

All roof water goes down hill

Water is diverted around the structure

14 permies.com/t/1356 (French drain)
15 permies.com/t/23442 (Mike Oehler's book)

That was easy. I simply pointed it uphill instead of downhill. Now the wraparound ditch gives us all of the perks that we get in a conventional home and everything that lands on the roof goes downhill to where it isn't bothering me. The important thing to note is that I have now fixed all of the water problems (sound effect for a cheering crowd goes here). And when I say that I did it, I really mean Mike Oehler did it (sound effect for a cheering crowd goes here also).

Now, you may be thinking: "Gee, great design. No water in my house, but all I've got to look at is the back of a hill instead of my beautiful downhill view. Wofatis suck." Well, now I'm going to poke a big hole in the downhill side so that I can still get all of that amazing view. The secret ingredient is a small gable roof attached to our existing shed roof:

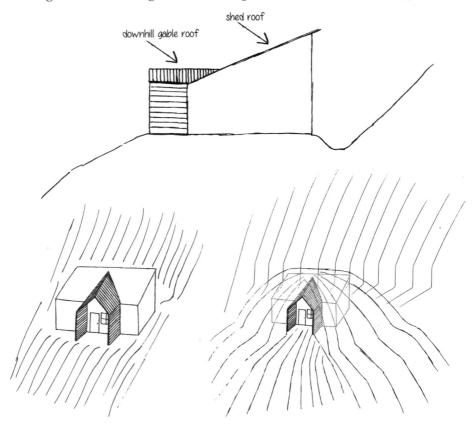

Water that reaches the house from the uphill side is diverted by the ditch that is below floor level. Any rain that falls on the roof will drain to the downhill side. Now we've got light coming into the building from both the uphill and downhill sides, AND we won't wake up to find our mattress floating in a flooded bedroom like we're in some sort of cartoon.

A Freaky-Cheap Home That Doesn't Look Freaky-Cheap

There are a lot of manufacturers out there who proudly proclaim that their houses are much cheaper than the average. It turns out that, with manufactured homes, you usually get what you pay for. The house *looks* cheaper than the average home – not the kind of place I would like to live in. My goal with the design of the wofati is to provide a more luxuriant space at half the cost of a conventional home.

Oh yeah...when I said earlier that Mike Oehler was trying to reduce material costs with his design...I kinda forgot to mention...Mike's original home only cost him $50 to build. Later Mike added on to that home to make it a little bigger and a little nicer. The cost of the addition: $500.

To be fair, Mike used a lot of scavenged materials. And if every person on the planet went this route, then there would be a limited amount of materials to scavenge. So the cost would be a little higher for things like new windows and plumbing parts. Still, even in that case, we're talking about the ability to build a house for only a few weeks' worth of wages. Yes, weeks – not years.

To illustrate how this might be possible, let's do a ground-up comparison between a wofati and a conventional home.

The first part of building a conventional home is the foundation. The foundation usually rings in at around a third of the total cost of a home. A wofati is a type of pole structure, so it requires no foundation.[16] There's roughly a third of the price gone.

Next, there are the exterior walls of the structure. Building a conventional home involves bringing in a lot of materials: framing lumber, nails, insulation, vapor barrier, plywood, drywall, etc. These materials all have a cost to them. In a wofati, the shell is made of trees cut from the land, a thin waterproof membrane, some dirt, and some wood duff. Materials cost: maybe a couple hundred bucks for the membrane.

Topping off the structure is the roof. Like the foundation, the roof is also roughly a third of the cost of a conventional home. Again, we're looking at lots of imported (read: costly) materials. And if you wish to do a standard "green roof," the cost of the roof increases by a factor of ten! But Mike's design and the design of the wofati are such that if you are willing to sacrifice skylights and the need for gutters, the cost of your roof will be less than a tenth that of a conventional roof! For materials, we're still looking at trees cut from the land, a thin waterproof membrane, some dirt, and some wood duff. Again, just the cost of the membrane.

Of course, not everyone wants to build their own house. Fair enough. But then you're probably going to have to pay someone to build it for you. My hope is that the comparison between a wofati and a conventional home painted a picture that suggested not only reduced materials costs, but reduced labor costs too. For example, drilling a few post holes is going to require much less labor than pouring a concrete slab, or, even worse, a damp, smelly basement.

Most of the labor for a wofati is going to come from log prep – harvesting trees, removing the bark, and bringing them to the building site. This can be a long process, but I think there are ways we can speed this process up significantly (e.g. harvesting the trees in early spring makes the logs easy to peel). Once the logs are prepped and ready, there is labor involved in erecting the structure and then it's mostly some time with an excavator for assembling the envelope.

It sounds like we are now well on our way to reducing costs. My hope is that as we continue to experiment with building these structures, we can find ways to optimize the process such that the labor to build a wofati is far less than a conventional home. And since the materials cost is extremely low, a wofati would be a beautiful, freaky-cheap place to live. And if that isn't enough, let's talk about how the structure may not need any heat or air conditioning...

16 permies.com/t/15615 (pole structures)

Using the Heat from Summer to Heat Your Home During the Winter

The shell of Oehler's structure has a waterproof membrane around it. In his book, he talks about using polyethylene (a clear or black plastic sheeting) for the membrane. Later, he started using EPDM (pond liner), which is thicker and less prone to having holes poked in it – but it is also more expensive. We hope that someday we'll figure out a way of doing this with purely natural materials. This membrane keeps any moisture from coming through the soil and into the house. That said, if there is a heavy rain or melting snow, the dirt that is just on the other side of the membrane is often wet.

Remember how straw doesn't have much insulative power, and yet a straw bale wall is considered to be far more insulative than a conventional wall? That's because it is so thick. The R-value per inch of a typical straw bale wall is rated between 0.94 and 2.68. For comparison, the R-value per inch of fiberglass batts is 3.1 to 4.3, but they are often much thinner. Looking at our green roof, the R-value per inch for dirt is roughly 0.05 when wet and 0.33 when dry. Six times more insulative when dry!

After I had stumbled upon Mike Oehler's stuff, I found a copy of John Hait's book called *Passive Annual Heat Storage*.[17] In that book, John appears to extend Mike's ideas to include a cheap means to completely eliminate the need to heat the structure. On top of dry dirt being six times more insulative than wet dirt, dry dirt also has the ability to retain heat for a really long time. Hait's book goes into a lot of mathematical detail on this, and he concludes that if you have 20 feet (~6 meters) of dry dirt, you can carry the heat of summer all through the cold of winter. Thermal inertia!

Well, I don't want to have a house that is 20 feet deep, and Hait doesn't suggest that. Instead, wrap this much dry dirt around more than half of the house. He has done this more than once and the result is a home that requires no heat. Hait's initial experiments were with homes in Montana – a great place to test heating strategies!

Incorporating Hait's research into the wofati design, now you have a layer of structure (R-2.5 to R-5), membrane on the structure, about eight inches (~20 centimeters) of dry dirt (R-2.64), about four inches (~10 centimeters) of wood duff (R-5), another layer of membrane, and then 20 inches (~50 centimeters) of wet dirt (R-1). This brings our roof R-value to about R-11 or better – pretty good! On its own this might not seem like much, but there's also a healthy dose of thermal inertia.

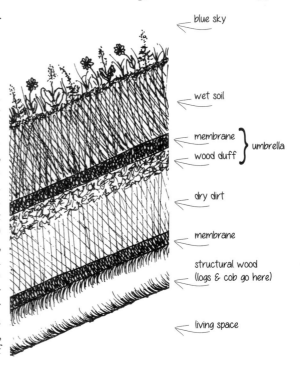

blue sky

wet soil

membrane } umbrella
wood duff }

dry dirt

membrane

structural wood (logs & cob go here)

living space

17 permies.com/t/50585 (John Hait's book)

Lastly, John Hait's book is called *Passive Annual Heat Storage*, but what the title leaves out is that this design also brings a great deal of cooling in the summer. I think the phrase "Annualized Thermal Inertia" is more accurate.

The Strict Definition of "Wofati"

Woodland

Oehler-inspired

Freaky-cheap

Annualized Thermal Inertia

So...W.O.F.A.T.I. But even though it is an acronym, I prefer "wofati." Ahhh... the joys of making stuff up...

Since I made up the word, I get to define what it means. If anyone is going to call their structure a wofati, I hereby require it to meet the following criteria:

1. Every drop of rain has a complete downhill soil path and never encounters a roof edge.

2. There are two layers of membrane. The lower layer, which hugs the structure, and the upper layer, which defines the thermal mass that surrounds the structure.

3. The uphill side has an open trench to move water around the structure.

4. The uphill side has a roof that extends at least five feet (~1.5 meters) beyond the exterior wall.

5. There are at least 8 inches (~20 centimeters) of dirt between the two layers of membrane. There are at least 16 inches (~40 centimeters) of dirt on the top layer of membrane.

6. The inner pole structure is made of logs.

7. No treated wood is used in any of the structure.

Further, if anyone is going to call their structure a wofati house, I hereby require it to meet the following additional criteria:

A. At least 35% of the uphill wall is glass or some other material that allows light to pass through.

B. There is a large gable roof on the downhill side with 35% or more glass or some other material that allows light to pass through.

C. The house is NOT "underground." This is an above-ground pole structure with a thick earthen roof.

A Modification for a Year-Round Freezer

One of the potential additional applications of wofati design is a wofati freezer.[18] We've already talked about using the heat from summer to heat your home during the winter.

18 permies.com/t/46478 (freezer wofati)

This is basically the same idea except backwards. A wofati freezer uses the cold from winter to keep things frozen throughout the summer.

While a wofati house is suitable for hot or cold climates, a wofati freezer is only going to work in a place where it gets really cold in the winter. It will include a pluggable vent tube that runs through the core of the thermal mass. The idea is to open these tubes for the coldest four months of winter and let the heat escape to the outside air. For the rest of the year, the tubes are plugged to reduce the amount of heat transferring into the mass. In order to keep the mass cold, it helps to have a big mass. The upper layer of membrane should cover at least five times as much square footage as the available square footage in the structure. With this in place, it should be possible to store food year round with zero ongoing energy inputs.

Chapter 31
Natural Swimming Pools

In some areas, nearly everyone owns a swimming pool. It's a place to cool off on a hot day and a great space for kids to play with their friends.

On the list of things that we really need in life, a swimming pool doesn't rank very high. It's a major luxury item. A standard swimming pool might cost fifty thousand dollars or more to build and thousands of dollars a year to maintain. They are built with tons of concrete, heated with gobs of power from the grid, and filled nearly to the brim with toxic gick to keep them "clean."

Rather than saying that everyone should live without one, I wish to embrace the luxury that comes with having a swimming pool and come up with ways to make it healthier, more enjoyable, and cheaper to build and operate at the same time.

Enter natural swimming pools.[1] These beautiful pond-like constructs are divided into two areas: the swimming area and the cleaning area. In the cleaning area, the water is naturally cleaned by aquatic plants and wildlife. The clean water is then returned to the swimming area where it is enjoyed by people who appreciate that they are not swimming in gross pond water.

I think it's possible to build a natural swimming pool for less than one tenth of the cost of having a conventional pool installed. No concrete, heated by the mighty power of the sun, and no toxic chemicals or artificial filters required.[2] Plus, it's a back-up reservoir in case there is ever a fire. It's hard to see why most people wouldn't want one of these.

Keeping the Water Clean

Have you ever seen a pool where people have let it go? They stop treating the water and they stop cleaning it. What happens? Typically, a layer of green pond slime forms on the surface. This is algae. Our mission is to create beautiful clear water that has no algae – without using chlorine.

Some ponds will have a powerful algae problem too.[3] And yet, some don't. So our recipe will be to come up with ways to have something pond-like without the algae.

A compost pile is made of "carbons and nitrogens." Algae loves the nitrogens: poop, rotten green plant matter, dead bodies – all the stinky things that are rotting. You

1 permies.com/t/7994 (natural swimming pools)
2 permies.com/t/66884 (more natural swimming pools)
3 permies.com/t/105834 (algae problems)

could also think of these things as nitrogen-heavy fertilizers. These are the things that make some plants grow big and dark green.

There are three ways to take the nitrogens out of the mouths of the algae (om nom nom):

1. Feed it to something else before the algae has a chance.

2. Offer the nitrogen a big carbon source so it can do the composting thing. Nitrogen is a little weird that way – it would far prefer to do the compost dance than the feed-the-algae dance (this is called "nitrogen immobilization").

3. Have such a huge amount of water exchange that there isn't opportunity for algae to set up camp in our spiffy swimming pool.

To take the nitrogen out of a pond, the old-school technique was to throw a few bales of straw into the pond. That is a lot of carbon which will activate nitrogen immobilization. Of course, today there is a 99% chance that the straw contains persistent herbicides which will make your growies sad (and we are depending on those growies to filter the water – more on that in a moment)! Take the extra step of making certain that the straw is organic. Similar tricks include throwing logs, or the root mass of a large tree, in the pond (side benefit – lots of hiding spaces for small fish).

Our approach works a bit like a freshwater aquarium. A super-freaky-big aquarium. Without glass. And you get to play with the fishes. There's lots of plants and gravel and a way to move the water through the plants and gravel. Plants such as cattails, duckweed, and bulrushes take up excess nitrogen and other funky bits, as do zillions of bacteria and other beneficial critters in the gravel. At least 40% of the surface area of the pool is dedicated as the cleaning area – the bigger the proportion of cleaning area, the cleaner the water will be.

One way that some ponds get a huge algae load is that there is an overload of ducks, fish, or livestock – all contributing that funky algae food. Light stocking leads to clean water. Heavy stocking leads to comedy.

The next important thing to take care of is to increase the amount of oxygen in the water.[4] Oxygen is vital in ensuring the survival of all of the plants and little critters in the water. Plants give off oxygen, but only during the day. At night they consume oxygen. And, without enough oxygen in the water to support them, most of the plants will be dead by morning and the water will get gross quickly.

A creek is loaded with oxygen as the water moves and is constantly getting turned over and over so that all the bits of water get exposed to air – then that oxygen-rich water can pour into your pond. But, since most natural swimming pools don't have a creek, it is up to you to come up with an artificial substitute.[5] A moment ago, I mentioned emulating the water filtration system of a freshwater aquarium. And that had a pump. Once we have a pump, we can fiddle with the water so that the pumping can make a micro waterfall that adds oxygen to the water!

A better approach is one presented in David Pagan Butler's video *Natural Swimming Pools: A Guide to Designing & Building Your Own*.[6] Instead of a water pump, he used a bubbler like you would find in a fish tank. The energy cost is very low. And the bubbler causes the water in the pond to circulate gently, which is much better for the plants and the little critters than moving the water with a pump. The coolest thing about this system: a frog can go through it unscathed! It is possible that, if your oxygen

4 permies.com/t/14405 (increasing oxygen)
5 permies.com/t/33162 (trickle tube)
6 permies.com/t/55998 (David Pagan Butler)

needs are low, you might be able to get by with a pump (water or air) wired directly to a solar panel – something that runs just during the day.

Avoiding the Ice Bath

These solutions are for summertime swimming. Winter swimming will require augmentation with a rocket hot water heater and/or solar hot water and/or something else.

Our filter will make half the pool surface have very shallow water (just a few inches deep) with plants. This leads to a lot of heat collection. This alone will probably work for most people.

Sepp Holzer uses a technique of setting large, dark-colored boulders (weighing several tons each) into a pond with good sun exposure. The boulders soak up the heat and slowly release that heat over several months. The greatest sun exposure is in May, June, and July, carrying the heat into August and September. The addition of a sunscoop around the pool will also help to keep more of the sun's heat in the area.

Adding a layer of insulation around a pool can help dramatically in very cold climates. I would like to suggest using some of the ATI ideas presented in chapter 30,

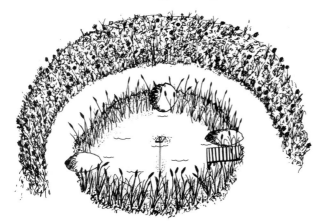

especially the idea that dry dirt is six times as insulative as wet dirt. Unfortunately this approach requires a waterproof membrane of some kind, so I only suggest doing this if the other ideas aren't enough for a warm swimming experience.

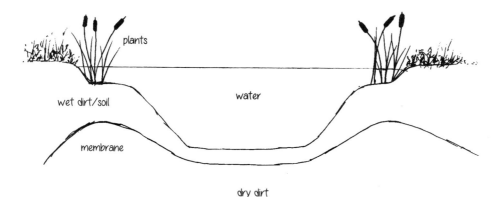

plants

wet dirt/soil

water

membrane

dry dirt

How Do I Build One? Gimmie! Gimmie Now!

While there are going to be many different designs for natural swimming pools, most of them are going to fit into two categories based on the site conditions: pool-esque and pond-esque.

Conventional swimming pools have vertical walls. If you don't have very much space (like in the city, for example), then you're going to need super steep walls in order to be able to have a swimming area with the depth you are looking for. This approach costs more than the pond-esque model because dirt doesn't really like being vertical, especially dirt with water lapping up against it.

Instead of cement walls, I would like to suggest cedar or black locust logs. Cedar will last far longer underwater than in the air. And black locust will last more than 50 years out in the weather – I suspect that it will last more than a hundred years in this scenario. Just make sure you take the time to soak them in water long enough that they stop floating.[7]

Ponds can be lovely to swim in and don't have vertical walls. They are much easier to build and thus also cost less to build, but they do take more space.

The bottom of both models can be built in the same way. I wish to eliminate felt and EPDM as options for sealing the pond, so I advocate Sepp Holzer's approach instead.[8] The idea is that you bring in a really big and heavy excavator and use the bucket to dig and shape your pool. Then once you're done digging, put on the smallest bucket available and push the bucket down in such a way that the front of the excavator comes up. Repeat this across the entire pond and it should seal.

Now you just need to fill the pool, put in the plants, and enjoy a luxuriant dip on a hot summer day.

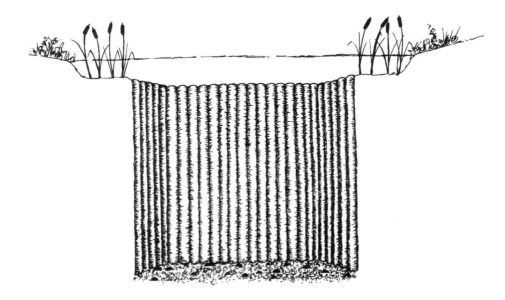

7 permies.com/t/waterlog
8 permies.com/t/196 (sealing ponds)

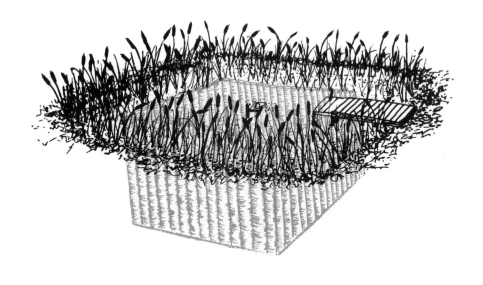

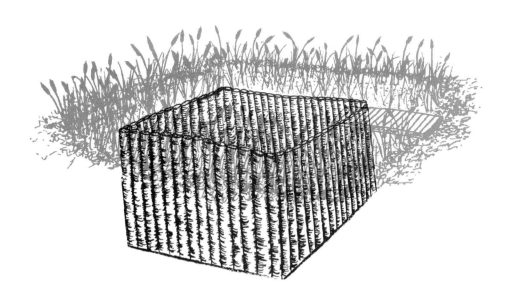

Part 6
Conclusion

Chapter 32
Hey! You Know What Would Be Cool?

Over your entire lifetime, you can sort out who to be angry at for making a big mess. You can tell thousands of people who to be angry at, and it will probably result in very little tangible change.

A few people will write letters, attend protests, or perform massive gestures. That might make a slight bit more difference – but that's a rigged playing field where the people who have an alternative view to yours are extremely well prepared to minimize your voice.

It seems our human nature is that once we have sorted out that there is a problem, we think we need to get the people who caused the problem to stop causing the problem. That makes sense. Of course, it turns out that "the problem" is about a thousand times more complicated than we originally thought. Nearly all of these massive problems are caused, indirectly, by us. By you. And when we get angry at "them" it turns out that we paid "them" to create this problem. And there were almost always alternatives, but we voted with our wallets for the bigger environmental disaster. Usually, due to clever marketing.

The problem is ourselves. We need to own our own shit. We need to clean our own backyard and stop feeding the monsters that are, in turn, harming (and even killing) our friends and families.

If we stop giving money to the monsters, they stop being monsters.

I once tried to share with an internet group how a rocket mass heater is the most environmentally friendly way to heat a conventional home. An anonymous person objected, pointing out that nothing is as clean as electric heat. What this person was missing was knowledge. There it is. The most important thing in solving all of the world's problems: Knowledge! Knowledge is the difference between drudgery and strategic action. Knowledge about the problems, and knowledge about the solutions. If we are going to ask a hundred million people to help solve these problems, we need to openly share the problems *and* a set of spiffy solutions that can be done at home.

Remember "The Wheaton Eco Scale"?[1] There is another observation I need to share. Most people at level 2 are confident that the scale pretty much ends with a handful of superstars at level 4. I think the only reason that people are not aware of levels 5 through 10, is that there is not a multimillion-dollar advertising campaign for the things at the higher levels.

1 permies.com/t/scale

For example, the rocket mass heater is a massive leap forward in solving problems. Ernie Wisner has built over 700 rocket mass heaters, and he was deeply involved in their development.[2] He's pissed. "When I was a kid, my mother told me that if you build a better mousetrap, the world will beat a path to your door. She lied. As is, the rocket mass heater solves so many things for so many people. And there is huge room for optimization. But the world appears hyper focused on trivial things. A toy will come out and become an overnight sensation – effortlessly. And a handful of us will put thousands of hours of effort into getting the word out about rocket mass heaters, and the response is relative silence."

Switching from electric heat to a rocket mass heater can displace a carbon footprint more than permanently parking 7 cars. An electric car has half the carbon footprint of a gasoline-powered car. So a rocket mass heater can reduce a carbon footprint by as much as 14 Teslas.[3]

You might not buy a Tesla this year, but you have probably researched it a bit. And you've probably talked to a friend or two about it. That's progress! Knowledge of a solution!

You might not build a rocket mass heater this year, but you can take some time to learn about them. And maybe you can visit with some friends about them. That's 14 times more progress!

It seems clear that people are willing to work hard to make things better for everybody – yay! But…their passion and effort seem to be mostly in light bulbs (which actually make things worse), or electric cars (which make things better, but not nearly as much as they hope). Maybe those wonderful, passionate people would be more effective if they knew about more solutions. And maybe the next time someone famous makes a movie about global problems, they will tack on a little something about rocket mass heaters and gardening.

Most Americans have racked up a lifetime of debt. Decency mandates paying those debts. Hundreds of millions of decent people commute to a job five days a week to whittle away at those debts and try to not feel so much like a slave to their past choices.

Many people go to their job, day after day, with a feeling of "I have to." I hope that with the ideas in this book, that feeling has changed to "this is part of my bigger plan." And that in a few years you can retire to a Gert-like world where your days are filled with the phrase "Hey! You know what would be cool? …"

2 permies.com/t/40993 (Ernie Wisner)
3 permies.com/t/43271 (heat footprints)

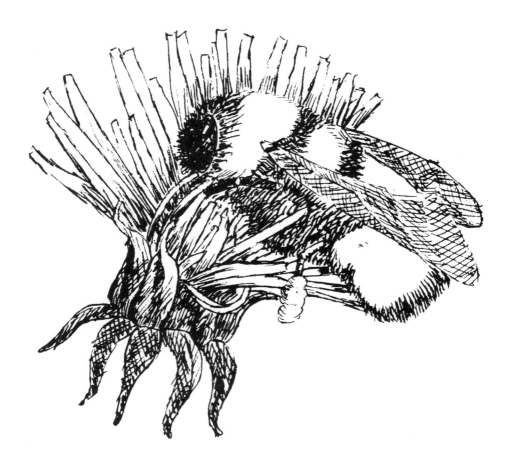

Appendices

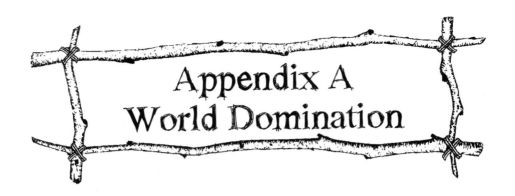

Appendix A
World Domination

Did somebody give you this book? We have designed this book with the idea that the person reading it is NOT the person that bought it. We sell this book by the dozen at

permies.com/bwb

We're not asking for donations for our cause. We are trying to make a stack of books freaky-cheap so that folks might be able to convey a philosophy set which might result in a stronger positive change than being angry at bad guys.

Special tip: For each book you give away, you might want to fold a corner of a page or put a bookmark in that says "This is the part that I think is most important for you." Or maybe fold the corner and write, in bright red ink, "This is the part I most desperately want you to read! Pretty please with sugar on top!"

Appendix B
Tabular Summary
of Solutions

Condensing huge conversations into a few numbers leaves out a lot of "it depends," but the hope is that this table gives a general idea of the impact that many of the solutions presented in this book can have.

Solution	Annual CO₂ Offset (Tons)	Annual Petroleum Offset (Gallons)	TFD Offset (Pounds)	Luxury Factor	Cost	Savings
Switching from a gas to electric car (for comparison)	2	500		+1	$40,000	$500 per year
Turning your thermostat down to 68°F while on electric heat in Montana	3			-1	$0	$150 per year per home
Using a "smart" thermostat to turn your heat down at night while on electric heat in Montana	3.5			-0.5	$100	$200 per year per home
Switching all your lights to LED in Montana (for comparison)	0.04		-0.1	-0.5	$100	$2 per year per person
Using electric micro heaters to cut 20% off your heat bill while on electric heat in Montana	6			-0.2	$100	$300 per year per home
Using electric micro heaters to cut 50% off your heat bill while on electric heat in Montana	15			-0.5	$200	$750 per year per home

Solution	Annual CO_2 Offset (Tons)	Petroleum Offset (Gallons)	TFD Offset (Pounds)	Luxury Factor	Cost	Savings
Using electric micro heaters to cut 80% off your heat bill while on electric heat in Montana	23			-0.8	$300	$1200 per year per home
Using electric micro heaters to cut 80% off your heat bill while on natural gas heat in Montana	7			-0.8	$30	$1000 per year per home
Switching to a rocket mass heater from electric heat in Montana	29			0 (+1/-1)	$400	$1250 per year per home
Heating with a conventional wood stove in Montana	4.5			-3 (+1/-4)	$2000 per year if buying wood	
Switching to a rocket mass heater from a conventional wood stove in Montana	4		+3	$400	$2000 per year per home	
Getting a smaller hot water tank	0.5			-0.2	$400	$40 per year per home
Going pooless	0.25		5	+1.2	$0	$120 per year per person
Using cold water and line drying for laundry instead of hot water and a dryer	4			0 (+0.5/-0.5)	$0	$200 per year per person
Living in community while still commuting to a regular job and buying most of your food from the store	3	150		0 (+4/-4)		$7000 per year per person

Solution	Annual CO_2 Offset (Tons)	Petroleum Offset (Gallons)	TFD Offset (Pounds)	Luxury Factor	Cost	Savings
Replacing toxic household cleaning products with better alternatives			45	+2	$10	$250 per year per person
Using cast iron instead of teflon			10	0	$50	$50 per year
Using diatomaceous earth for bug killer instead of poison			5	+1	$20 per year	$80 per year per home
Growing 10% of your own food	1	50	4	+1	$20 per year	$400 per year per person
Growing 50% of your own food	5	250	17	+2	$50 per year	$2000 per year per person
Growing 90% of your own food	10	450	33	+3	$150 per year	$3600 per year per person
Growing 90% of your own food plus 10% of the food for ten other people	19	950	76	+4	$250 per year	$5000 per year
Growing 90% of your own food plus 90% of the food for ten other people	110	5000	396	+4	$500 per year	$32,000 per year
Sequestering 1 ton of wood from your yard	1			+1	$0	$400
Building a full greywater system instead of a conventional system			1		$3000	$150 per year per person + $5000 if building a new system anyway

Solution	Annual CO_2 Offset (Tons)	Petroleum Offset (Gallons)	TFD Offset (Pounds)	Luxury Factor	Cost	Savings
Using a willow feeder or dry outhouse			1	0 (+2/-2)	$300 to $1200	$150 per year per person
Growing a mowable meadow instead of a conventional lawn	0.5	8	15	+2	$0	$100 per year per yard
Building a wofati instead of a conventional home heated with electric heat in Montana	30		25	+3	$25,000 less than a regular home	$1500 per year per home
Building a natural swimming pool instead of a conventional swimming pool	1.5		10	+3.5	$45,000 less than a regular pool	$3000 per year per pool

Acknowledgments

We started this book thinking that Shawn would grab 30 articles I had written and mash them into a quick eBook in about 100 hours. After about two months, we were so passionate about massaging every sentence to be "the best" that we decided to play the long game. After thousands of hours, we have something smaller and better. We are on pins and needles waiting to see if it is worthy of a greater audience — thus proving all the extra work was worth it.

We decided on "self pub." If we truly understood how much work that meant, we might have been less certain about that. Printing, shipping, layout…did you know there are about five different kinds of editor for a book?

In the end, we got by with a little help from our friends. A lot of friends. You really don't think of how many friends you have until you start to make a list. More than a hundred people chipped in with bits and bobs of polishing the content of this book — making excellent arguments for re-phrasing, or better qualifying a number, or sharing a bit of additional info. I cannot imagine books being written without so much help.

I think that this final product is extremely well-polished because of all the wonderful people who took a large slice out of their lives to help.

I need to start the acknowledgments with the biggest thanks going to the volunteers who manage the forums and all the other things that make up the permies.com community. Without their help, I would never have suggested the idea of the book, nor would Shawn have learned of that suggestion. The community at permies.com is the brightest light in my life.

I (Paul) want to thank Jocelyn Campbell for constantly spoiling me throughout the process and hearing my crazy approaches, and being the rock doing all the money fondling.

Shawn would like to thank Andrea Klassen-Koop for the amazing amount of patience and support she showed as this project dragged on for many more months than originally planned. Words do not suffice to express the depth of his gratitude.

Thanks to Esther Allerton for massive support over many years, providing a foundation for this project. Thanks to Devaka Cooray for the mountain of modifications to the permies.com software that allowed us to try things with the Kickstarter for this book. Thanks to Tracy Wandling for upgrading our book from mere words to something that has more life. Thanks to Raven Ranson for giving feedback on nearly every version of every chapter, plus writing a whole new book to offer as a stretch goal in the Kickstarter! Thanks to Fred Tyler for helping us find a respectful path on our two vegan chapters.

A huge thanks goes to all the people who gave significant feedback to help shape this book, whether they were experts sharing advice on a particular subject, authors sharing tips and tricks learned writing their own books, or people who just cared so much about this project that they spent hours upon hours of their lives helping to make it awesome: Bill Crim, Thomas Rutledge, Nicole Alderman, Victor David Sandiego, Rob Roy, Bill Compton, Willie Smits, Alan Booker, Bill Kearns, Richard Kutscher, David Pagan Butler, Jacqueline Freeman, Jacob Lund Fisker, Jeanne Boyarsky, Mark Tudor, Julia Winter, Jay Angler, Dave Burton, Mike Jay, Terrance Grundy, Paul Loewen, JP Peters, Jennifer Richardson, Jade Hays, Ryan Barrett, Nina Jay, Daniel Ray, Michael Judd, and Joshua Myrvaagnes.

Thanks to Jack Spirko, Steven Harris, David The Good, and David Huang for getting the word out, so effectively. Thanks to Kenji Dyck for creating a fun and engaging video for our Kickstarter campaign. And thanks to Matt Veith for introducing us to Kenji.

Thanks to the people who took the time to give numerous suggestions, detailed feedback, or words of encouragement that often ended up with us changing something for the better: Renee Lawver, Kerry Rodgers, Daron Williams, Tony Jennings, Thomas Rubino, Jeremy Franklin, Jane Bartlett, S.M. King, Anne Miller, James Freyr, Sarah Kaplan, Greg Harness, Dan Boone, Lesley Verbrugge, Vernon Inverness, Jerry McIntire, Sonja Draven, Rudy Valvano, Inge Leonora-den Ouden, Kenneth Elwell, Davin Hoyt, Greg Martin, Jarret Hynd, Tina Hillel, Wayne Fajkus, Ash Jackson, Chad Sentman, Susan Stone, Bryan Paul, Richard Gorny, Jonathan Krohn, Sue Rine, Gurkan Yeniceri, Rita Bliden, Roberto Pokachinni, Josephine Howland, and Miles Flansburg.

Thanks to the people who put the time in to understand what we were attempting to say and give constructive feedback: Sara Hjalmarsson, Jon Stoski, Erwin Decoene, Karen Donnachaidh, Juan Sebastian Estrada, Estar Holmes, Kyle Neath, Thomas Rubino, D. Logan, Stephen Lowe, Cory Arsenault, Alex Ojeda, Stephen B. Thomas, Sarah Milcetic, Anthony Cooley, Joy Oasis, Kim Arnold, Philipp Mueller, Dennis Barrow, Gail Saito, Barton Mazza, C. Letellier, Bryan Beck, Phil Swindler, Glenn Herbert, Brian L. Cooper, Bernetta Putnam, Cat Melvin, Hal Hurst, Juliana Hess, Peter George, Dave Smythe, Chad Pilieri, Ed Hoffman, Robert Jordan, Mark Campbell, Klaus Kaan, John Copinger, Dakota Brown, Brett Mathews, Susan Pruitt, Kate McRae, J Spears, Larry Jackson, Beth Cromwell, Dick Chase, Lisa Petrillo, Natasha Todd, Kyle Bob, Molly Kay, Ian Giesbrecht, Deb Stephens, William Wallace, Marco Banks, Katie Duncan, Steve Lansing, Mandy Launchbury-Rainey, Judith Browning, Penny McLoughlin, John Strohl, Simon Scott, Loxley Clovis, Craig Dobbson, John Suavecito, Isa Delahunt, Luke Iseman, J Webb, Rebecca Norman, Henry Jabel, Mussa Gladden, Jennifer Richardson, Letitia Davis, Dave Powell, Katie Young, Nathan Toombs, Tim Bermaw, Kady Carlson, K Rawlings, Cindy Skillman, Jess Dee, Kathy Mason, Heather Strouhal, S Wesley, Melissa Bracy, Tim Skufca, Chris Kott, Mick Fisch, Lucrecia Anderson, and Lina Joana.

GOOFBALLS KEEN ON WORLD DOMINATION

Our most glorious supporters!

Greg Martin,
biochar.com

Bill Crim

Katie + Carl Young
BlueFeatherHomestead.com,
mac nuts plus!

Christine de la Tabernacle,
Duchess of the Vanishing Point

JessB

JP Peters,
a votary of Paul Wheaton
& Jacob Lund Fisker

Polly Jayne Smyth

Jocelyn Campbell

Raven Ranson

Thomas Rutledge

Esther Allerton

The wind beneath our wings…
The propulsion fuel in our jet boots…
The massive crowd carrying us, kicking and screaming, into awesomeness…

These are a few of the 2768 brave souls that supported our Kickstarter campaign without having read the book. Thanks for your faith in us! We hope it was worth the six-month wait!

TMC	Ryan Brown	Radhe Webster
Al K	Bruce Love	Warren Whippo
JimW	Jeff Dible	Steve Mezsick
TAWF	Rich Masta	MB & E Markey
Debu	M.Gudewicz	Bradley LaMar
JessB	AndymAndym	Jim Marangoni
SZÖSZ	Mark Tudor	Kona Paradise
Nepeta	Jon Stoski	Kenneth Rough
MRKOCH	Candy Loam	Vaclav Hnizda
Bill 3	Atlas Reid	Dwight Bishop
Giroux	Pete Lundy	Anny the Grok
dooora	Patricia Z	Jason Learned
Murphy	Dirty Diana	Evel Martinez
Matito	Roadscholar	Karol Hartley
WeRGods	Chad Meyers	Permie Spirit
Gene Ey	Lori Diamos	Murray Urreta
PennyMc	Ry Thompson	Madeline Wood
Mike VP	Paul Binfet	Dave Thompson
paulzg30	Masterknife	Michael Buyer
Jessamyn	Zach Cohoon	The Aldegolds
Jenjamin	Luke Iseman	Eric T. Mings
Turon RS	Jesse Jones	Sojourner4869
MesaLisa	Lovely Rita	Tatiana Zimina
Mike Arr	John Dorsey	KJIH in Canada
Ourelsie	Andrew Rule	stevie gibbons
Tuna Rod	Andy Strunk	Thadius Marcus
peatlane	Todd Feltner	Derek Murawsky
Ben Birby	Mike & Jamie	Shelley M Hall
Bill Crim	Brett & Dana	Donald Kenning
Tonzarama	Kyle Burdick	Corey Scribner
_(ツ)_/¯	Walton Hoops	Joshua J Feyen
Gypsy Deb	viva Bill M.	Rastus Jackson
AC Howard	Off Grid Guy	Famille Landry
Senstless	Gusty Rhodes	Lars Woltemade
mahBarker	Aaron Thrift	Craig and Lory
Zoie Yell	Andrew Moore	Austin Grizzle
Alex Pine	King Richard	Ann Socolofsky
JOAT, MOS	Joe Gesualdi	Florian Hübner
Ginny Bee	Michael Hawn	Little Bad Bird
Eato Grot	Michael Wood	Dominic Crolius
Cool Fire	Paul Pittman	Michael Tullius
Anonymous	Nick Onaboat	circadian.ninja
Tom Lucas	Jason Schalk	Kevin Derheimer
Bret Mayo	Sara Acridge	Jason Mainville
Kit Hammes	Steven Every	Peak Prosperity
Chris Sugg	Rudy Valvano	Diesel Dog Dehn
Thanks Mom	EmilyFantasy	Austin Driscoll
Doug Barth	David Powell	Carrella Werner
Roz Snider	Jeff Carlson	Greg MineralFix
Jay Skiles	Jimmy Graham	Sound Living NS
J.R. Haley	Heino Konrad	Cassie and Jojo
Wild Yeast	Yinergy Yoga	Frank E Polk Jr
fraser day	Brian Stretch	Boondocks Hawks
Derek Cate	Popsicle King	@HomesteadHubby

Atreyu Guiltron
Jeremy Weathers
Scott Nicholson
T n L Goodspeed
William Donovan
Christopher Ray
Charlie Skyhorse
Jonas Atterbring
Mz ArtificeSmith
Gary Pietrocarlo
Sky Prairie Farm
Steve Biernesser
The Desert Fleet
Crafty Lady Lyda
David Sonday Jr.
Paul Trentham MD
Caroline Sharkey
Buck Shot Rogers
The Leach Family
Huxleberry Finn.
Robert S. Vibert
The Devine Famly
Natural Outliers
tspCreatives.com
www.iwilltry.org
Ponderay Permies
Michał Czarnecki
Coon Creek Ranch
Booky McBookface
www.campchet.com
Andrew Willerding
Polly Jayne Smyth
Ellison Family WV
Kerry JustTooLazy
Piper Iggy Hammer
Daniel J Brieck Jr
krs_ticopuravida!
Homer & Val Smith
GrownFolkTalk.com
MyKyHomestead.com
PermaDave Kincaid
Creighton Samuels
Drager Farms, LLC
Flamingo Sundries
Stephen Vermilyea
Stella of the Forest
Ten O'Clock Acres
Drum Journey Jeff
Annie Daellenbach
Pfaffke von Oilsjt
Justin K. M. Fournier
D. Walter Marcil, Esq.
Rommel M Gonzales
Dah-veed Ahn-drews
Plant Person Pivik
Dominic Schultheis
Renaissance Woman
CJ@CruxHomes.com
https://edible.estate/
Desert Forest Farm
Aunt Megan's Herbs
Mr. (Amazing) Ward
MQ the Magnificent
www.megmitchell.ca
Stacy Savola Wright
Creaking Alder Farm
Jennifer Richardson

Richard Breitenbach
The marvelous nines
Guerrilla Oeschgers
Mehron loves Nefeli
Richard Kicklighter
The Scoggins Family
John "Dizzle" Wiley
Kathryn della Porta
Maeve of the forest
Christian L. Schwarz
Prickly Hedgehog Gal
better world in deed
Keanu Charles Reeves[1]
Seeker and Starstuff
Stephen Greszczyszyn
Hazelwoodville Farms
Isibéal Ní Luachráin
Dana the Denominator
Sir Chickie of Chucks
Frog Farm Deb & Steve
Timothy (Nick) Baglin
Josh & Jenny Feathers
Gray and Katie Turner
Mr. Nola agin canajun
Mike & Megan Koeniger
Marc Live Free or Die
PugetSoundPrepper.com
www.dreamsofclay.com
Jeff The Happy Higdon
Sam DuBois in Ecuador
India and Emma Parker
Cast Iron Farm, Sooke
James from Canada eh!
Matt and Rose Carroll
Hungry Hawk Homestead
elements design.build
Thomas Duncan Thompson
Tyron & Jamie Baltazar
Unit Y314 Black Jaguar
Jeffrey Haney Hiscocks
Dave Burton the Permie
Diamond K Welsh Ponies
Short Family Homestead
Fergiesonian the great
Provenpermaculture.com
Eric and Jamie Maschuck
Chris & Hollie Holcombe
Tigercello Permaculture
Shillims from Norn Iron
Yoda likes permaculture
www.serenarosemusic.com
Forever Young Movements
Tom & Amanda Bowersox
CARLOSG in Amsterdam
The Responsible Citizen
Robert D. MacMorran III
Charlotte B and Mikel S
Food, Fire, Family, LLC
Greg Martin, biochar.com
Kind Pharm in Arco Idaho
The Mackay clan in Japan
Nadine West (Austin, TX)
Rick Baue "It starts here"
Justin 'credible' Gerardot
"Ralph" the Wonder Llama
American Craftsman, Utah
Cowgirl Carmen & Cohorts

www.EmpoweredHerbals.com
Derek and Danielle Monger
In memory of Petey Wilson
Myles & Haley Steinhauser
John-Eric Colley Robinson
John Conner - Coop Janitor
Col Nick Norton (299 Days)
Diamond B Farm and Rookery
Lydia Ashleigh Baumgardner
Wendy the Crazy Plant Lady
In memory of Ed Richardson
The Cult of the Giant Shoe
Dallas Smith of the Cariboo
Steve Stamhuis & Wendi Weir
In memory of Cynthia Siarny
For Juniper, for the future
Johan Bergknut Skåne Sweden
Bubba Schott Miles Farm "42"
Bushels 'n Pecks, Branch, MI
Supreme Bunny Lauren Paolini
Buried Hippies the Card Game
Froggy Hollow, Belfast, Maine
Masterherdsman Triple Kocurek
Lazy Hollow Farm Lakeland, FL
Thanks Jack, You're a Jerk. - Karla
Jephph the Great and Powerful
John Sechrest, Graand Poobaah
In memory of Mary Ellen Clarke
Anton & Maja Puščavar Šinkovec
Oscar from Pagosa Springs, CO.
Mycotylium of the Rot Revelers
Robin and Duff at Miradar Farm
Michael C Roth - @michaelcroth
SRFNY - Stoney-Ridge_Farms_NY
Ben Hawkins - Hawkins Road Farm
The Korneliussens - Memphis, TN
Niveragain from Niverland Ranch
Jimbo from Tomahawk Permaculture
Winston P Cat and the Tricky Boys
In Honor of Bobbie and Sam Groves
Mike Bruhn USMC - Drinker of Beer
The Cram Farm-Kris and Ginny Cram
Rob Bond III - Bond Fluidaire Inc.
Derek Gibbs - Our Shared Adventure
Becky Weisgerber the Mushroom Lady
Mike-and-the-Clear-Creek-Pine-Nuts
Jonathan Jocelynn Alexander Arbizu
Marlaleta C. and Erik L. Pehoviack
Plum Crazy Farm at the Holmes Ranch
Laureen Sue Magyari - Sourdough Sue
Dave Rossa, The Wall Of The Achaeans
Mike "Liberty Innovations NC" Heindl
Pasquale DeAngelis of DeAngelis Farm
David "OklaHomesteading.com" Burklin
Brian, Gail, Matt, Tricia, and Inara
Northern Permaculture farming at -40
Our posterity, Claudia & Amelia King
Vernon Inverness ~The Triumphant One!
The UNVAUNTED UNDAUNTED6!
Sarah, the Quail Queen of Eldredge Rd
Whiskey Flat Farms, Highwood, Montana
Boundless Permaculture - Derek Kirbow
Reverend Baker of greenfaith Ministry
Klemen - yurts & stuff - www.jurta.si
For Bob & Mary Thomas of Johnstown, OH
Locust Creek Haven for Woodland Plants
Kyle Bob - World's Handsomest Engineer

1 We opted to not verify the authenticity because it might not actually be him.

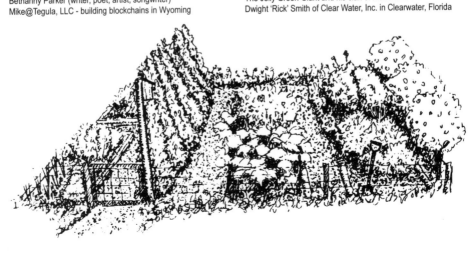

In loving memory of Dr Jasper Caper ~ healer and published poet
Somebody's going to have to go back for a sh_tload of dimes....
Jon Hutson, Esq., Warden of Cats and Principal, Global Media Max
Daniel Spinelli and Briana Bisordi of Fermento Mori. Be Here Now.
Sarah & Peter Milcetic, Better with Thyme Farm, Shepherdstown, WV
YAHUAH (YHVH) and HIS SON YAHUSHA are LORD of HIS creation
Ditch USD/EUR/RMB for money-less currency that resists consolidation
Andrew Personette - andrewpersonette.com - broad scale Permaculture
Progontheranch.com where musicians and music lovers enjoy farm life!
Maeve: Hope is important but so is action. Mummy and Daddy love you!
nwshearing.com, shetlandsheep.com, northwestshepherdess.com

Denise Spencer Servant of YHWH and caretaker of the Garden at Shiloh
A pledge for Lynne Watson Snyder, who loved and wrote, Just Trent
Nina von Feldmann with Tender Wellness and Happy Healthy Homes
In memory of Eleanor & William Webb, my gardening grandparents
M and Nico, Lesbians and Permaculture Goddesses Extraordinaire
Everything is born; everything dies. In-between is living. LIVE WELL.
René & Lesley VERBRUGGE, Permaculture les Vallées, Normandie, France.
Family Overmeijer, Paul, Judith, Maximus, Roxanne, Rocky, Nina & Suzie
Sweet Unborn Taters, Azilah, Jen, Mr Giddy, and Louisiana Permaculture
Matt Winters, Overlord of Wintershaven Permaculture demonstration site
In memory Craig Smith, who showed me how to to imagine a better world.
Strategic Planning for Small Nonprofit Organizations www.missionmet.com
For Artemis Bee and Sirena Shale, the two best friends anyone can have.
Bill Erickson - the Wardog of Montana who eats breakfast with Spiderman

in memory of Virgil R. Hanford great grandfather to Virgil A. J. Hanford
^..^ You are what you eat - so don't be fast, cheap, easy, or fake. ^..^
In Memory of Megan Elizabeth Stucky - Michael and Missy, Millenium Farms
For my grandfather Turner Mayfield, who set an example that has guided me
Anita Unrau, Animal Communicator and author of my non-traditional journey
Laura Rutherford, Benevolent Dictator and Lead Workhorse at Alchemy Acres
MidcoastMaine Crew-Linc,CJ,Mike/Ash,SAM!,Madi, TJ, Ant, Nick/Wren, BRIAN!
In memory of the conventional gardening & plants that previously suffered
In memory of Robert Louis Tognoni who loved fishing in the great outdoors
Jenny Katz Freescaling.com learning to improvise using your musical nature
David Huang doer of stuff at www.theartistshomestead.com and davidhuang.org
Santiago Miranda - Molinos Verdes de Moringa Costa Rica - Haisel y Gustavo
Terence Lie: "Make the world better through self awareness and connections"
Grow swamps, feed our bats! Microbats are Cute! {\^.^/} ~BattyFarmer.com.au
Mountain House Permaculture (BlossomMountain Dairy Goats & Grey Fox Garden)
The Conscious Chef - permaculture, cooking, foraging, gites, french pyrenees
In loving memory of Walter and Leta Bondy. Life long gardeners. (V. Hanchon)

Goodspeed and Score, with Sage Stone Botanicals' citronella insect repellent
Scott Cousland, Holistic Advocate. Founder of One Big Sky & Utopia Unchained
In memory of Bernard Moitessier who unknowingly did permaculture on Poro-Poro
Eric "The Mad Farmer" Tolbert can be found at https://tinysustainablelife.com
Kissing Cousins Farm, "Keeping farming in the family". Derek and Tina McKenzie
Matthew and Katie Bucktrout, La Ferme du Beau, France lafermedubeau.weebly.com
For a better world that Giovanni, Diana, and Margaux de Valdivia may enjoy it.
Overlord Russell Graves, Self Declared Emperor of Helser (syonyk.blogspot.com)
Make this world a better place, wow! Thank you from H2O2 Design & Development.
Russell Venditto, gondolier and Spanish teacher extraordinaire; Providence, RI
Miss Tatym Sunshine: happy days inspired by this excellent collection of ideas!
Katy Jean Guidone 3/20/1970-3/6/2018 - Amazing wife, aunt, teacher, and runner.
Nick Vreeland - and Jack Spirko is a jerk for telling me about this Kickstarter
Follow the Collignon Family permaculture homestead @The_Homesteading_Herbivores
Dave Forrest & Guillermo Gomez Urzelai, registered permaculture designers (PRI)
In memory of my Grandparents, Dale and Mary Hester, on whose farm I fell in love
Kristy Gonyer Building a better world in Black Hills, SD toadhollowhomestead.com
Compost a conflict into fertile relations, joy & regrowth. EscapeYourChains.co.uk

Gretchen & Dale Demmin, Return to Roots Farm – be kind to and respect each other
Gredloc Bronder- Dont gaze into the abyss, unless its blk coffee, then drink up!
The Survival Podcast Zello Channel - Where the cool kids hang out zello.com/tspn
Cate/Mark Mawson: Cdn source 4 cloth diapers https://www.bamboodiapersonline.com
www.CreativeOasis.LIFE- Journeying in Faith, Permaculture, Home, Health & Family
Master of Eastern and Western Medicine in All Points North to South, Daniel Coho
Tiala Wilson. You really can change the world if you care enough~M Wright Edelman
cotoverde.org Home Scale Sustainability Solutions Permaculture•Science•Engineering

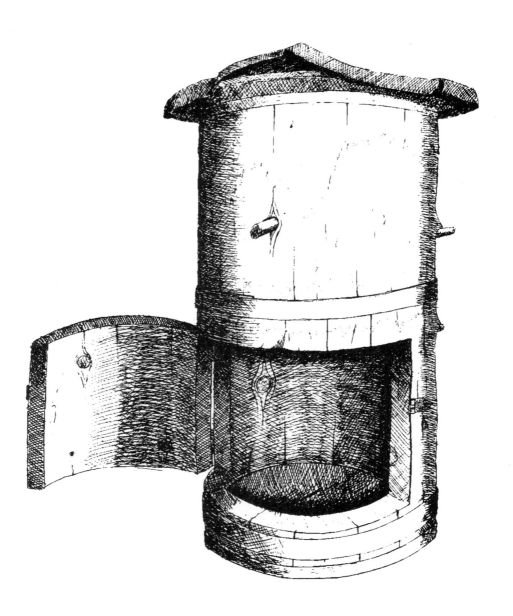

164

About the Authors

Paul Wheaton

Paul is a giant doofus in Montana who is bonkers about permaculture. He won't shut up about permaculture. On and on, every day…it's annoying. He has gone so far as to make a 3-DVD set that is just about the earthworks for permaculture gardening. And not only did he make a 4-DVD set about rocket mass heaters, but he made ANOTHER 4-DVD set about rocket mass heaters. Why on earth do people need 8 DVDs about something so simple? If you think that is ridiculous, take a look at his 177 hours of video of a full Permaculture Design Course and Appropriate Technology Course. Then there are the cards. Okay, the permaculture playing cards are pretty cool.

Before all of that, Paul created hundreds of podcasts, YouTube videos, articles and other bits and bobs about permaculture. That should have been the first sign, right there, that health professionals should have stopped all this. That, or his 26,000 forum posts at permies.com. And he has at least that many at his other site, CodeRanch.com. Oh yeah, he used to be a software engineer before all this permaculture stuff.

Shawn Klassen-Koop

Shawn's passion for building a better world grew from many years of working at a summer camp. This time inspired awe and wonder for the natural world through many hours camping in the woods, paddling on a lake, or sleeping under the stars. Seeking to solve world problems with clever thinking, Shawn decided to pursue computer engineering as a career, where he learned the importance of good design and strong critical thinking. In time, he felt like modern technology was causing more problems than it was solving, and he started looking for a better way. It was then that he stumbled upon and fell in love with permaculture as a way to use his design skills to work with nature rather than against nature. Shawn was preparing to start his own homestead when he was faced with serious health challenges that prevented him from doing any physical work. It was during this time that the opportunity to work on this book came up. Shawn jumped on it, wanting to do whatever he could to share these ideas with others.

GOODMAN'S FIVE-STAR STORIES

MORE
TRAVELS

8 More Stories from Around the World
With TESTS to Help You Read and Write

by Burton Goodman

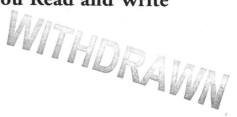

Glencoe
McGraw-Hill

New York, New York   Columbus, Ohio   Chicago, Illinois   Peoria, Illinois   Woodland Hills, California

JAMESTOWN EDUCATION

TITLES IN THE SERIES

Travels	Level A	Shocks	Level E
More Travels	Level A	After Shocks	Level E
Adventures	Level B	Sudden Twists	Level F
More Adventures	Level B	More Twists	Level F
Chills	Level C	Encounters	Level G
More Chills	Level C	More Encounters	Level G
Surprises	Level D	Conflicts	Level H
More Surprises	Level D	More Conflicts	Level H

Glencoe/McGraw-Hill

A Division of The McGraw-Hill Companies

Cover illustration: David Cunningham
Interior illustrations: Jim Abel, James Buckley, Sandra Burton, Yoshi Miyake
Acknowledgments are on page 122, which is to be considered an extension of
this copyright page..

ISBN : 0-89061-646-9

Send all Inquiries to:
Glencoe/McGraw-Hill
8787 Orion Place
Columbus, OH 43240

7 8 9 10 11 12 116 / 055 09 08 07 06